TENNIS

Strokes for Success!

Sports Illustrated Winner's Circle Books

BOOKS ON TEAM SPORTS

Baseball
Basketball
Football: Winning Defense
Football: Winning Offense
Hockey
Lacrosse
Pitching
Soccer
Volleyball

BOOKS ON INDIVIDUAL SPORTS

Bowling
Competitive Swimming
Cross-Country Skiing
Figure Skating
Golf
Putting
Racquetballl
Running for Women
Skiing
Squash
Tennis
Track: Championship Running
Track: The Field Events

SPECIAL BOOKS

Backpacking
Canoeing
Fly Fishing
Scuba Diving
Small-Boat Sailing
Strength Training
Training with Weights

TENNIS

Strokes for Success!

by
Doug MacCurdy
and
Shawn Tully

Illustrations by
Robert Handville

Sports Illustrated
Winner's Circle Books

Photo credits: Russ Adams: pages 48, 75, 79 (right), 81; Simon Bruty: page 136; Tom Ettinger: pages 134, 143; Andy Hayt: page 22 (left); Caryn Levy: pages 3, 16, 23 (right), 36, 41, 58 (top), 76, 78, 79 (left), 85, 92 (right), 101; Ronald Modra: page 100 (right); For *Sports Illustrated*—Melchior DiGiacomo: pages 62, 71 (bottom); Jacqueline Duvoisin: pages 33, 57, 67; Heinz Kluetmeier: pages 24, 44; Walter Looss, Jr.: pages 37, 88; Frank Micelotta: page 96; Manny Millan: pages 20, 28, 49, 50, 148; Steve Powell: pages 22 (right), 38, 74, 92 (left); David Walberg: pages 12, 23 (left), 58 (bottom), 68, 83 (top), 100 (left), 106, 122.

FIRST SPORTS ILLUSTRATED BOOKS EDITION 1994
Sports Illustrated Tennis: Strokes for Success! was originally published by Time, Inc. in 1988.

Sports Illustrated Books
An imprint of Madison Books, Inc.
Lanham, MD 20706

Distributed by National Book Network

Library of Congress Cataloging in Publication Data

MacCurdy, Doug.
Sports illustrated tennis : strokes for success / by Doug MacCurdy and Shawn Tully ; illustrations by Robert Handville.
p. cm.
1. Tennis. I. Tully, Shawn. II. Title.
GV990.M3 1993 796.342'2—dc20 93–28170 CIP

ISBN 1–56800–006–5 (alk. paper)

Acknowledgments

We're indebted to Thomas Ettinger, director of Sports Illustrated Enterprises, for his encouragement, guidance, and superb editing.

Thanks also go to the United States Tennis Association's Education and Research Center in Princeton, New Jersey, for providing us with important research materials, and to its director, Eve Kraft, for enriching our knowledge of tennis over the years.

We are also grateful to Steven Kraft for his help.

Contents

Introduction 13
Taking Stock 14
Choosing Equipment 17

1. Ground Strokes 21
Four Pointers 21
Developing Consistency, Depth, Spin, and Pace 25

2. The Forehand 29
The Grips 29
The Ready Position and Shoulder Turn 31
The Stroke 32
Placement 37

3. The Backhand 39
The One-Handed Backhand 40
The Two-Handed Backhand 45

4. The Serve 51
Developing an Effective Serve 51
How to Serve 53

Correcting Errors 59
Adding Spin 60

5. Volley and Overhead 63
Playing Net 63
How to Volley 65
Volleys Requiring Unusual Footwork 69
Variations of the Volley 70
The Overhead 73

6. Special Ground Strokes 77
The Return of Serve 77
The Approach Shot 80
The Half-Volley 82
The Passing Shot 84
The Lob 84
The Drop Shot 86

7. Continental and Western Styles 89
The Continental Style 90
The Western Style 93
Unorthodox Players 95

8. Competition 97
Your First Tournament 98
Dealing with Tournament Conditions 98
Maintaining Fitness 103

9. Singles 107
Playing the Score 107
Paper Percentages and Personal Percentages 108
The Serve 109
The Return of Serve 115
Backcourt Play 115
Mid-court Play 117
Net Play 120

10. Doubles 123
General Techniques 123
Setting Up a Doubles Team 124
The Roles of the Players 128
Play After the Serve and Return 132
Alternative Formations 134

11. Practice 137
The Basic Principles of Practicing 138
Practice Requirements 140
Drills 142

12. Positive Thinking 149
Sportsmanship 150
How to Avoid Choking 154
Dealing with Discouragement 155

Appendix: Scoring 157

Sports Illustrated
TENNIS
Strokes for Success!

Though tennis players may look different today compared to a few decades ago, all style their strokes from a common foundation of good form and solid technique.

Introduction

During the past few years, we've had the privilege of teaching tennis all over the world, and we have found that what passes for tennis clothes, a racket, and a court differ as much from country to country as do the words for "Good shot." Our tennis adventures have taken us from country clubs in the United States where children debate the subtle differences between graphite and fiberglass rackets, to a rubber plantation in Liberia where kids scamper barefoot around courts paved like roads, hitting balls with wooden breadboards from the family kitchen.

Everywhere we've gone, however, we have found that good players, no matter what their gender, nationality, size, or age, look pretty much the same stroking a tennis ball. Good form is universal. And by analyzing the tried-and-true strokes and tactics all good players share—and leaving out quirks and personal eccentricities of style—we came up with a model for a good tennis player.

It is this basic technique on the court that we want to teach in this book. Each chapter you work through should take you a step up the tennis ladder and a step closer to the ideal or model game. As you progress, you'll focus on different parts of the model. As a beginner, you should simply try to develop model strokes. As a sound, experienced player, you will aim higher, striving not only to polish your strokes but to develop sound tactics as well. Although the beginner has a lot farther to go than a good player, each is pursuing the same ideal and can deviate from it only so much and still forge ahead.

What do you have to do to learn? First of all, you don't have to be a good athlete, although it helps. We believe anyone who has: (1) the ability to hold the racket in one hand (or even two), (2) the desire to learn the game, (3) the patience to practice, and (4) the means to enjoy it can learn to play tennis or learn to play it better. We want to show you how.

This book can be divided into two parts, the first covering the basic strokes in detail, the second dealing with supplementary strokes, tactics, and psychology. As a beginner, you should study chapters 1 through 6, put the book down until you've mastered the strokes, then read chapters 7 through 12. Advanced players can skim through the early chapters and concentrate on the later ones. Intermediates should read all chapters in detail.

To keep things simple, we've described how to hit the ball from the standpoint of a right-handed player. Left-handers must reverse the instructions. It should be noted, however, that left-handers do have a big advantage over right-handed players, especially righties who aren't used to playing lefties. This is probably why, as the years go by, more and more world-class players are lefties. Tactics for left-handers are discussed in chapters 9 and 10.

TAKING STOCK

Some of us want to play tennis for its social aspect—the getting together with family or friends—some of us for the exercise, some to have a few laughs. Others find their weekly game comes to mean every bit as much to them as a tournament final would to a professional. To most of us, though, the game's importance lies somewhere in between. We would rather win than lose, but our self-esteem doesn't suffer too much if we lose, and we don't find winning to be the solution to all of life's problems.

In short, most of us want to play tennis because it's fun. And common sense tells us that if we could play better it would be even more fun.

To advance to a higher level of play, you must first take stock of where you are. Then you can decide where you would like to be. For most people, getting to a higher level of play means not only perfecting (or even just acquiring) a sound arsenal of strokes but also learning and being aware of good tactics.

The Tactical Approach

The term tactics refers to the specific pattern of shots you work out beforehand in order to win a point. This amounts to a series of choices. When returning a short ball, for example, it's sometimes appropriate to hit an approach shot, sometimes a drop shot. Strokes must have accuracy, spin, and power to execute tactics, but the tactics themselves come first; we must decide what we want to do with the ball before we determine how to hit it.

Since all of us do not hit the ball in exactly the same way (nor should we want to), individual style has come to have an important place in tennis. Chet Murphy, director of tennis at the University of California, calls the variation among good strokes the "range of correctness." Although good players hit the ball very differently, they use similar tactics, patterns of play that have won enough matches over the years to be considered classic.

Tactics are what differentiate mediocre players from good ones. Too many players are terrific hitters but not such terrific players, simply because they don't know how to play a point or why they play it the way they do. They may look great warming up or taking lessons, but their quest for perfect strokes becomes an end in itself. They end up losing to savvy competitors who may have far weaker technique.

Developing your game along tactical lines will give your hours spent practicing or playing on court a purpose and will help you realize what strokes you need to change or acquire in order to keep improving. In the second half of the book we'll discuss "strategy"—by this we mean your game plan for winning a match, not just a point.

How Long Does It Take to Get Better?

If you have never played tennis, the curve on your improvement chart will probably bolt upward at first, even without much practice. Some lucky people have the right hand–eye coordination to play tennis the first time out. Their experience in other sports automatically applies to tennis. Conversely, some athletes who have the speed, strength, and endurance to excel in other sports do not have a feel for the racket work, which is what the beginner's game is all about. If you are an average athlete, you should be able to play tennis well enough to have great fun within six months of taking your first swat at the ball. All you need do is practice for one or two hours three times a week.

If you are a novice, instruction can speed up your progress a great deal by reinforcing the principles you learn in this book. Lessons get you out on the court regularly, introduce you to practice routines and to other students with whom you can do the drills outside of class, and sometimes—if the teachers are enthusiastic—get you excited about learning. Group lessons are every bit as efficient as individual lessons, and they cost far less. A good group teacher presents the fundamentals so that everyone in the class can absorb them at once. You will improve more quickly in the first few lessons simply by going through the practice routines with students of your own caliber, routines you can also practice outside the group. In recent years, an ever-expanding network of courses for teachers has elevated the quality of instruction. Obviously, the

Frequent practice may not give you as powerful a serve as, say, Stefan Edberg, but it will help add an important component to your game—consistency.

quality of teaching varies from place to place, but there are good programs offered through parks, schools, YMCA and YWCA recreational programs, camps, and clubs.

The Importance of Practice

A tennis teacher, no matter how good, cannot work miracles. You must spend time practicing outside of class. If you are unable to find a partner during the first few weeks of lessons, you can reinforce what you've learned by swinging the racket in front of a full-length mirror or hitting against the garage door. If instruction is unavailable, watch carefully how a good player hits the ball. You can even learn without a good player to watch. While on a tour of West Africa, the late tennis great Arthur Ashe found a young boy with flawless strokes banging away in Cameroon. To Ashe's amazement, the boy said that he had learned his strokes from a book. He went on to become the first black African touring pro.

If you play enough to keep your newly acquired skills, say once a week, you can enjoy the game for the rest of your life. If you wish to keep improving, good instruction will usually help, but time and proper practice are what really make the difference. (Practice techniques will be discussed in detail in the second half of the book.) When you practice, remember to follow two rules: (1) Play at least three times a week, and (2) spend at least a third of your time practicing rather than playing games.

If you are dedicated, becoming a good player is easier than you might think. Young players often compete in tournaments a year after picking up a racket. And with daily workouts, a well-coordinated adult can play relatively consistent, aggressive tennis within a few months.

CHOOSING EQUIPMENT

A good player could beat a bad player, even with a snowshoe. No single piece of equipment is going to propel you through the levels of play. And don't think the only reason your opponent can beat you or play better is because of a racket (or, for that matter, any other piece of equipment). It just isn't so.

The Right String

Up until a few years ago, tennis purists argued that, no matter what you paid for a frame, it was the strings that were important—they did all the work; the frame merely held the strings in place. Recent technological innovations have changed all that. Today, when buying a racket and strings, you should think of them as equally important, each one enhancing the performance of the other.

For years, natural gut was considered by serious players the string of choice because no synthetic string was as responsive. Not anymore. Today there are synthetic strings on the market that very nearly duplicate gut's feel and elasticity, yet cost less, and are far more durable and longer lived than gut. With space-age sounding names like Tecnifibre and Sterlon, these synthetic strings come in a wide range of materials, textures, gauges, and colors. Which is for you?

If you're a weekend player, go nylon. It's still the cheapest and will last a long time played on only once or twice a week. If you're a more serious player, try one of the more gutlike synthetics. The string you choose might be made of specially-treated nylon, boron, Kevlar, graphite, fiberglass, or composites of these, but will generally be of a thinner gauge than a low end nylon string, have more resiliancy, and "grip" the ball better. If you're a very serious player, consider one of the textured synthetic strings. It will increase your feel for the spin of the ball—particularly important if you like to put a lot of topspin on your shots (more on topspin later). Of course, if you're a serious traditionalist, natural gut is still there—if you want to pay the price for it.

No matter what your level of play, as a rule you should restring your racket—and install a new grip—as many times a year as you play a week. That means if you play only once a week, you need only restring your racket annually. On the other hand, if you're a very serious player using a thin-gauge synthetic string, you might find yourself actually breaking strings from time to time, thus speeding up your restringing schedule.

String tension plays a role in being well equipped. General rule: the looser the strings, the greater the power generated, but at a sacrifice of control; the tighter the strings, the greater the control—up to a point (beyond which the racket becomes boardlike and mis-hit shots feel uncomfortable). If you're prone to arm problems or want more power, string somewhat looser and perhaps avoid stiff string and racket materials such as graphite or boron. If you're a hard hitter but want control, string tighter. Generally, midsize rackets (the most popular kind on the market today) are strung at tensions between 55 and 65 pounds, while oversize rackets (the slightly less popular alternative) are strung at 70 to 80 pounds. If you're unsure of your capabilities, you're best off following factory recommendations printed on the racket's throat and ordering a medium tension.

The Right Frame

The advent of oversize and midsize rackets in the last decade has rendererd the traditional, standard-size racket virtually obsolete. Today you can buy rackets in a bewildering variety of styles, shapes, and materials, in varying degrees of oversize or midsize.

If you're a weak player, or primarily a serve-and-volleyer, or a doubles player, consider an oversize racket. With its huge "sweet spot" (the area, upon impact with the ball, of zero torque, or twist), the oversize racket provides a tremendous advantage in returning difficult shots, and can transform a duffer's mis-hit shots into winners. If, however, you're looking for a more all-purpose racket, a midsize is probably your better choice. Its sweet spot is still large, but its reduced size improves the racket's playability, making ground strokes easier to control with it.

Assuming, thereafter, that the racket's size, weight, grip, and balance suit you, there is only one other major factor in racket selection: degree of flexibility. At impact, a flexible racket bends a bit and then snaps back to its original position. The racket does a little of the work for you. Be careful that it doesn't do too much of the work, for if it's too flexible, you lose control. A stiff racket provides no extra power, but if you hit the ball solidly, it does give you excellent control. Today, space-age synthetics have more or less completely eliminated wood as frame material, along with steel and aluminum. Generally, rackets of graphite, boron, Kevlar, and ceramics—all popular frame materials these days—tend to be stiff; those made of fiberglass tend to be flexible. In between are composites of these materials, which tend to create frames of medium flexibility. Good players seeking to hit with a little more pace tend to choose slightly flexible frames, while players with plenty of power often select stiffer models. For most players, a composite racket with medium flex is ideal.

To pick a racket, start by looking at a few models that advertise the flex you want, then try them out before buying. If you are about to purchase your first racket, take into account that you are a beginner, and avoid buying a model designed for a hard-hitting pro. Go to your local tennis shop—*not* your local discount house; the former will steer you to a racket that suits your game. Now *play* with the racket. You will get used to its feel in no time. In fact, your first racket is usually a tough ally to part with, even if it's an antique you found in your grandmother's basement.

DHL

1

Ground Strokes

In tennis, the object of the game is to hit the ball into your opponent's court once more than your opponent can hit it into yours. It's that simple. Many points end quickly with a winning serve or two missed serves (a double fault), but more often than not the point is won after a duel of "ground strokes." A ground stroke is a stroke made after the ball has rebounded from the ground. Although technically the return of serve and the half-volley are considered ground strokes, the word usually refers to shots made while the player is standing behind or near the baseline. Consisting of the forehand and the backhand, ground strokes are the foundation of a sound game.

FOUR POINTERS

Whether the ball comes to your forehand or your backhand, remember four things basic to all ground strokes: Watch the ball, prepare early, keep your body in balance, and follow through.

Watching the Ball

Of these four pointers, watching the ball is the

Sound ground strokes are the foundation of winning tennis. Here Martina Navratilova displays perfect backhand technique.

most basic. If you ignore the other three, your stroke may be awkward, but you'll probably hit the ball back; if you take your eye off the ball, you'll be lucky to deflect it off your racket frame. Focus on the ball from the instant it leaves your opponent's racket, and follow it until you can practically see its individual hairs. Watching the ball and early preparation go hand in hand; the quicker you see which side your opponent's shot is aimed for, the sooner you can turn and start your racket back.

Preparation

To a large degree, how quickly you prepare for the ball determines how well you play tennis. When a tennis instructor mimics the stroke of a champion for a beginners' class, some beginners may be able to produce a duplicate in a few moments. But as soon as the ball approaches with any speed, the novice is likely to freeze or produce some jerky travesty of the newly learned stroke. On the other hand, an experienced player would calmly turn the shoulders and make a seemingly effortless ground stroke. This all starts with early preparation. By the time the ball has traveled a few feet from the opponent's racket, a good player starts to turn to the right for a forehand, to the left for a backhand. In the same situation, an intermediate player may wait to turn until the ball has reached or crossed the net, a novice until it bounces on the court. (Preparation also means getting your racket back. We will discuss this later.)

Prepare early for all shots. On both forehand and backhand, the initial movement is the shoulder turn.

Body control and balance are all-important to proper shot-making. If possible, the weight should be on the front foot on contact (left). A few players, like Jim Courier (right), are able to maintain control of the body even though both feet are off the ground.

These differences in reaction time of the three categories of players are not just a matter of reflexes. Top tennis players may be superb athletes, but they also must prepare early. Practice will sharpen your reflexes, and soon you will automatically prepare early too. After seeing the same patterns of shots time after time, you learn to anticipate where the ball is going to go.

Balance

Once you decide to play the ball as a forehand or a backhand and start to move your racket back, you must get into a balanced position to make a good swing. At the point of contact, your body should be stable and leaning slightly forward in the direction you are hitting. Learn to stay in control of your body, even when you're not hitting from a perfect stance. Hit on the run only in emergencies. Otherwise, you'll find yourself in emergencies all the time. If you run and hit at the same time, your racket may jump or jerk as it moves forward and you will lose control.

Follow-through

Good balance, then, helps supply the fourth ingredient for good ground strokes, a smooth follow-through. The follow-through is that portion of the swing which occurs after the racket makes contact with the ball. When the strings of your racket meet the ball, they stretch or move backward. At the same time, the ball flattens against the strings. As the racket continues forward, the strings snap back to their original position and the ball regains its normal shape. This coupling of ball and racket *feels* instantaneous, but it lasts for longer than you think. It is possible to keep the two in contact for up to a foot. And the longer you can hold the ball on the racket, the better chance you have of directing it accurately. If this "carrying" effect of ball meeting strings were not so effective in directing the ball, you could probably play tennis just as well with a baseball bat.

The better the follow-through, the longer you can hold the ball on your racket. To direct the ball, the racket face must continue along the path you want the ball to follow. If the racket face stops for only an instant, the ball may go anywhere.

The other parts of the strokes are discussed in the chapters that follow, but none of them has nearly as much impact on your control as the follow-through. And control is the name of the game.

There is a good deal of variation in the styles good players use and the ones tennis pros teach. And though the way the game is played and taught changes every time a player beats the world with a "new style," this style is never altogether new. Every good player watches the ball, prepares early, has a good sense of balance, and controls the ball by keeping it in contact with the strings with a good follow-through.

All good ground strokes include a complete follow-through.

DEVELOPING CONSISTENCY, DEPTH, SPIN, AND PACE

Now that we have discussed the major ingredients in hitting good ground strokes, let's take a look at what you must do to keep your strokes effective in play.

Consistency

At most levels of play, consistency alone will make you a winner. If you can attack as well as defend, you are even more likely to win. Nevertheless, the winner almost always makes fewer unforced errors than the loser. Even in a championship match, the players are doing well to hit one winner for every three errors.

Surprisingly, some players get used to making an error after hitting a certain number of balls. It is as if they say to themselves, "OK, Sue, you've hit seven balls in a row and it's about time for this point to end." A player with a ten-ball limit will beat one with a limit of seven. It takes discipline to avoid panicking in the middle of a long rally. If you can hit fifteen shots in a row into the court, you should be able to hit a few more. Consistency comes from practicing the strokes, concentrating, and keeping calm. Don't try to kill the ball. Just keep it in play.

Depth

A deep shot is one that lands in the court within several feet of your opponent's baseline. Consistency and depth go hand in hand to produce good baseline play. Balls that land short are much easier to return and also allow your opponent to come in to the net and better control the point. Your goal is to hit deep shots consistently. It doesn't matter how hard they are hit, as long as they land deep. This keeps your opponent back, where the least damage can be done. In fact, a looping ball that bounces up around the shoulders is often more difficult to return than a crisply hit waist-high ball.

The importance of good depth is often misunderstood by intermediate players. They marvel when a good player hits a few shots that skim the net, overlooking the fact that *most* shots, the ones that make a good player so hard to beat, are going high and deep.

To hit deep in a baseline rally, aim your shots at least 3 feet over the net. On the run or off balance, you'll need 6 to 10 feet of net clearance, sometimes even more. Hit as high over the net for depth as you think necessary. You may not get the ooh's and aah's of the crowd, but you *will* get the points.

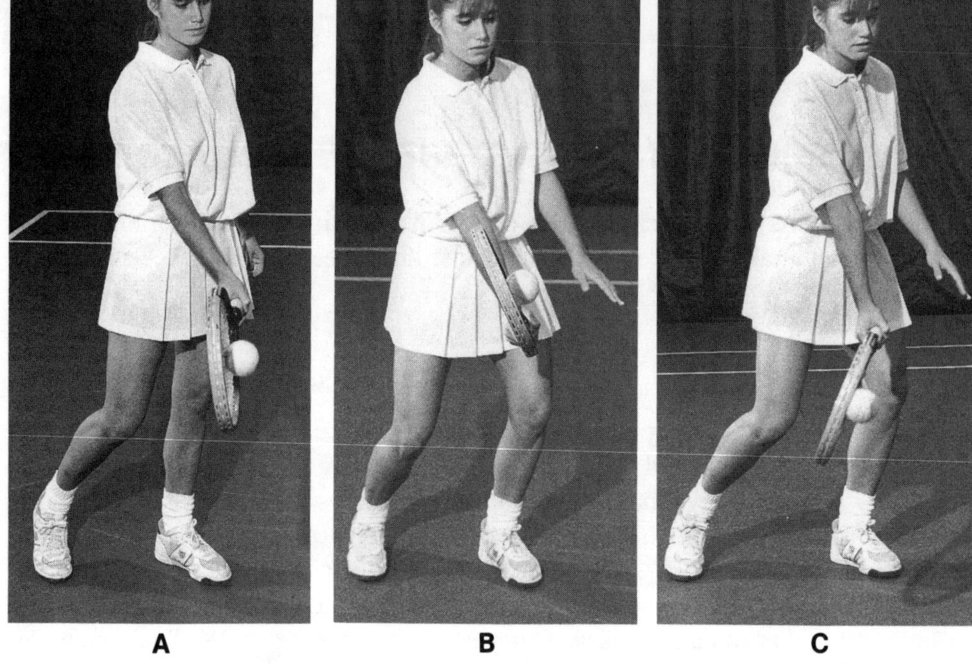

Fundamental to all strokes is the position of the racket face as it meets the ball. The racket face is said to be square or flat-faced when it is perpendicular to the ground. This position is used for most ground strokes. An open-faced racket, angled slightly upward, causes the ball to go high over the net (and probably out) unless considerable underspin is applied. A closed racket face, on the other hand, usually sends waist-high balls into the net unless plenty of topspin is applied.

Spin

Spin refers to the rotation of the ball as it leaves the face of the racket. There are three types of spin: topspin, sidespin, and underspin (also called backspin or slice). A topspin ball revolves forward, as if it were rolling down a hill; an underspin ball revolves the opposite way; and a sidespin ball revolves either to the left or the right like a top.

Hitting topspin ground strokes gives you a big advantage, since topspin makes the ball curve downward quickly, allowing you to hit the ball high and hard (and deep) without hitting it out of the court. If you have good forehand and backhand strokes, on which the racket travels from low to high, you will automatically impart topspin.

While you get topspin by swinging from below the level of the ball to above, you apply underspin by hitting from high to low. Use the underspin, or slice, sparingly, as a change of pace. These balls tend to rise or float, limiting how hard you can hit them without sending them out. The beauty of the slice is that, with little effort, you can take the speed off an oncoming ball and return it deep. As an added advantage, after it bounces, a slice often skids and stays low, giving your opponent a tough shot to dig out.

Sidespin is produced by starting the swing outside the path of the approaching ball and swinging across it, from outside in. The ball tends to skid, as on a slice. Sidespin shots are generally not taught by teaching pros, but they can be an asset, particularly as approach shots.

Since it is impossible to hit the ball time after time with no spin, a "flat" stroke is something of a myth. Most so-called flat hitters have a trace of spin on their shots. Flat shots have their advantages. Because you expend no energy on making the ball rotate, you can hit hard, penetrating shots. However, it is difficult to control the ball, since you must rely on gravity alone to make the ball drop into the court.

Pace and Speed

A ball is said to have "pace" when it moves fast after it bounces. A player who leans into the ball and accelerates the racket hits with pace. "Speed" refers to how quickly the ball moves through the air. It can be produced by a fast-moving racket alone. Players who flick their wrists at the ball and hit off the back foot can generate speed, but the ball slows down after it bounces and feels lighter against an opponent's racket than a ball hit with pace. Pace, then, is preferable to speed because it gives your opponent more to handle once the ball bounces.

The attainment of pace and speed are the last steps in your tennis development. Only when you can hit consistently deep, with some spin for control, should you apply pace.

The technique of hitting forehands and backhands is the subject of the next two chapters. But no matter how you hit the ball, remember to watch it. Preparing early and having good balance and smooth follow-through are also essential. Your goal should be to develop ground strokes with consistency, depth, spin, and, finally, pace.

But don't rush yourself. Strive to be a perfect beginner, a perfect low intermediate, and so on through the levels. You must crawl before you walk and walk before you run. By jumping ahead and trying to do things you are not able to do consistently, you slow your progress; you can even ruin your game. As you advance, you will find it infinitely easier to add to a solid foundation than to go back to the drawing board to completely revamp your game.

2

The Forehand

There is a range of forehand grips that a good player can use, but the choice of most teachers and top players is the "eastern" grip. Like its alternatives, the "western" and "continental" grips, eastern is a whole style of playing as well as a grip. The grip dictates the pattern of your swing and where your racket meets the ball: behind your left hip if your grip is continental, even with your hip if it's eastern, and in front of your hip if it's western.

THE GRIPS

Eastern Grip

Most teachers prefer the eastern grip because of its many advantages: It keeps the racket face perpendicular to the ground without forcing you to turn your wrist at the instant before impact to straighten it out; the palm is set firmly behind the racket, providing maximum leverage as you hit; it works well on balls of any height; and, finally, with an eastern grip you can hit topspin merely by swinging from below the level of the ball to above it. The eastern grip has one disadvantage: You must change it to hit backhands, volleys, and most other strokes.

Displaying his renowned concentration, Ivan Lendl prepares to unleash one of his lethal forehands.

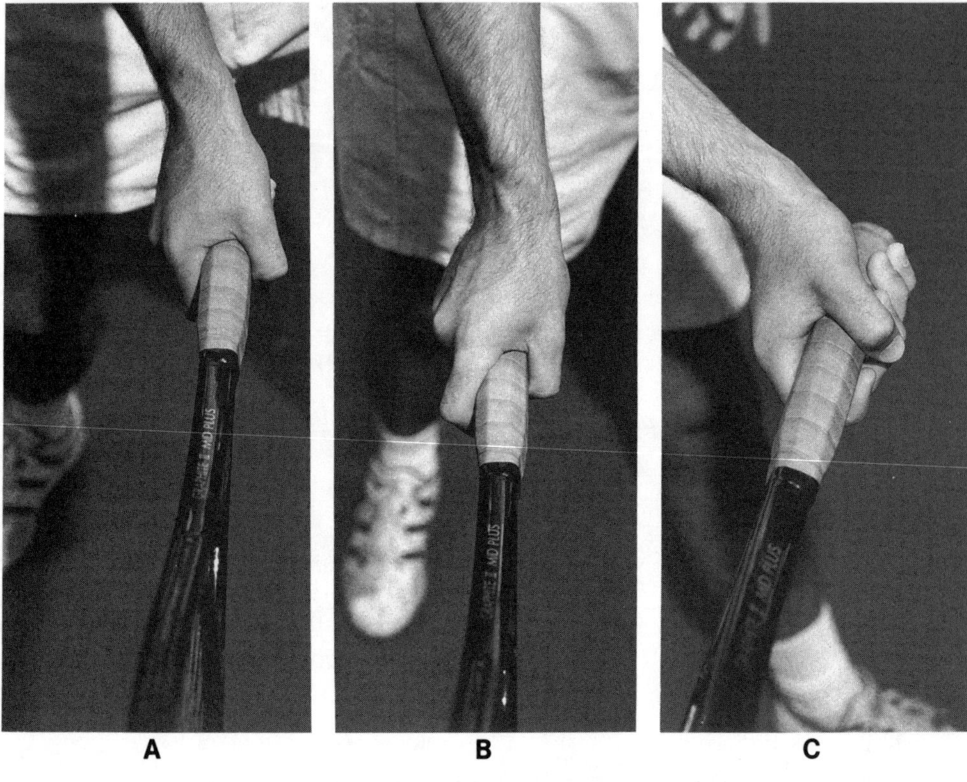

A B C

With the eastern forehand grip (left), the U formed by the thumb and index finger should be on the top bevel of the racket. This puts the palm of the hand behind the handle for leverage at impact. With the continental forehand grip (center), the palm is more toward the top of the racket than with the eastern forehand grip. With the western forehand grip (right), the palm of the hand is practically on the bottom of the racket.

With the eastern grip, the racket face is an extension of your palm. To find the eastern grip, hold the racket in front of you, cradling the throat in your left hand. Place your right hand flat against the strings and slide it down to the grip. Grasp the racket so that the thumb lies just above the middle finger and below the index finger. Spread the fingers comfortably, covering a good deal of the surface of the grip. If you bunch your fingers at the bottom of the grip, you may take a wristy "slap" at the ball, and the racket will tend to twist in your hand at contact. When you look down at your grip, the U formed by your thumb and index finger should be on the top bevel of the racket. Hold the racket loosely, squeezing it only as you hit the ball.

If you are just starting to play, use this grip unless it feels uncomfortable. If you have been at it awhile and wish to compare the grips, use the eastern as the starting point.

Western and Continental Grips

To find the western grip, turn your palm to the right, or toward the bottom of the handle, about half an inch. If you place the racket flat on the floor and pick it up like a frying pan, you have an extreme western grip.

To find the continental grip, move the palm to the left, or toward the top of the handle. Definitions of grips vary, but for our purposes a "full" continental grip is about the same as an eastern backhand. An eastern grip is sometimes called a "strong eastern" when the palm is set firmly behind the handle. Some players say this grip is "toward the western." Whatever you call your grip, it should be both comfortable and close enough to the eastern to provide the foundation of a good forehand.

THE READY POSITION AND SHOULDER TURN

After hitting the ball, get in the ready position and wait to see whether the return comes to your forehand or backhand. This means you should be "ready" to move to either side when the ball approaches. But don't exhaust yourself by crouching like a sprinter. Relax, be light on your feet, and lean slightly forward. If you are uncomfortable or find it a chore to straighten up from your ready position to hit the ball, stand up straight for a while.

To start the swing off well, pay attention to every detail of the ready position. Stand erect for a moment, holding the racket with the eastern grip. Take the racket shaft in the fingers of the left hand. The face of the racket should be perpendicular to the ground (not parallel with it), the right hand just below waist level and the top of the racket head about chest high. The racket tip may point straight ahead or slightly to the left. If the racket hangs down or points too much to one side, the stroke will suffer.

Leaving your left hand on the racket, turn your shoulders to the right. The racket automatically turns with you. If necessary, you could hit the ball right now. More backswing will add rhythm and power, but it is not needed to hit the ball over the net. How well you make the turn has a lot to do with how well you play. Strive to read the direction of oncoming shots as they leave your opponent's racket. The quicker you turn, the more time you have to make the return.

Let's look at the position of your feet. The right foot may pivot, pointing the toe to the right, or it may just stay in place. The hips may swing around less than the shoulders. If you have to take a few steps to reach the ball, run with your body sideways to the net.

A B

Your ability to make the shoulder turn and backswing early will determine to a great extent the level of tennis you will play.

THE STROKE

Backswing

The backswing should be a logical continuation of the ready position and turn. In the ready position, your racket head is about chest high. As you turn, the racket remains at the same height. If the ball you are returning bounces waist high, the head of the racket is a foot or so above the level of the ball. At this stage, the arm is about to take over the job of hitting.

The racket continues along the same chest-high path until it points to the fence behind you. The elbow, which has been close to your body since the waiting position, straightens out smoothly, dropping the racket head below the

Martina Navratilova displays perfect body control and preparation on her forehand.

level of the ball. Your swing should trace the capital letter C. The C motion gives you several advantages: (1) Your stroke is continuous and rhythmical, (2) you generate power naturally (almost like a wind-up in baseball), without a lot of muscle, (3) you can take the racket back smoothly and easily while running, and (4) you can easily raise the racket to handle balls that bounce unexpectedly high. The C motion may give you one problem, a tendency to take the racket back too high, causing you to be late on fast balls.

Instead of making the C, you could take the racket straight back. This works best if the racket head is lower than waist level in the ready position. If so, the racket just swings back and forth like a gate opening and closing. Or you could start in the normal ready position, with the racket chest high, and take the racket back diagonally below the level of the ball. Either way, you might save a fraction of a second, but by stopping the racket before bringing it forward, you lose the continuity and other benefits of the C.

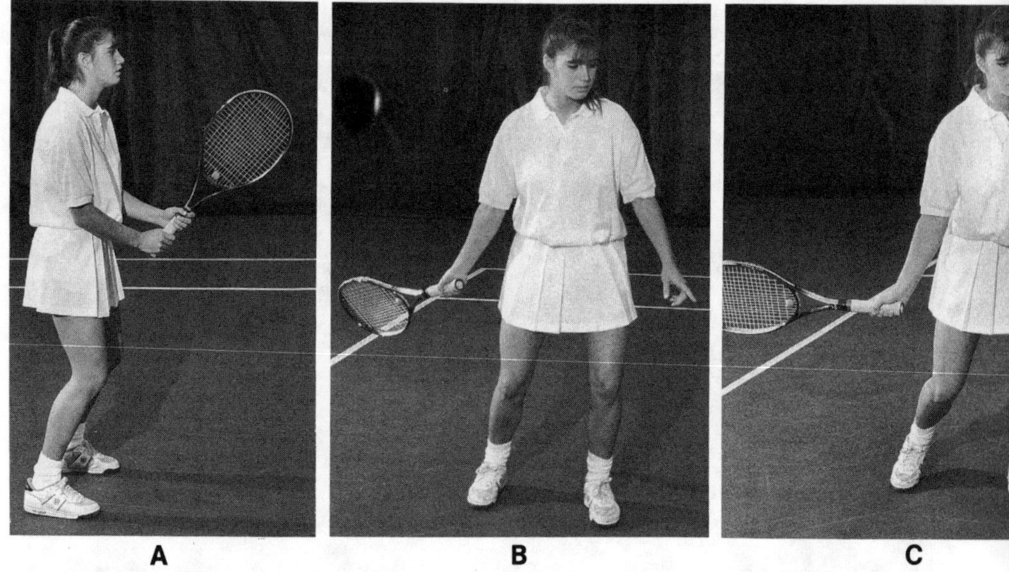

Forehand. From the ready position (A), the shoulder turn begins the backswing, which continues until the racket points directly behind you (B). The elbow straightens to drop the head of the racket under the ball (C) and the racket is brought forward to meet the ball at a point even with or slightly ahead of the left hip (D). On the follow-through the racket face is kept perpendicular to the ground (E).

Balance, Contact, and Follow-through

Your racket now starts forward and is about to contact the ball. Before hitting, try to step toward the oncoming ball with your left foot. This gives you a stable hitting base. Try to step just as your racket begins moving forward. If you can't step then, do it earlier—not later. It is better to hit off your right foot than to make a last-second step with your left.

Bend the front knee on low-bouncing balls. Bending lowers the racket to the level of the ball, which prevents "scooping" or "golfing" swings and keeps you in balance. Even on balls waist high or above, a slight bend at the knees can only help.

The racket moves upward, contacting the ball just in front of the left hip. For a bit more control and pace, accelerate the racket as it hits the ball. Remember, hitting upward gives you some topspin, an essential for control.

What you do while the ball is on the strings and just afterward determines how steady and accurate you are. Keep the racket face moving as long as you can in the direction you're aiming the ball. The racket keeps going until it points

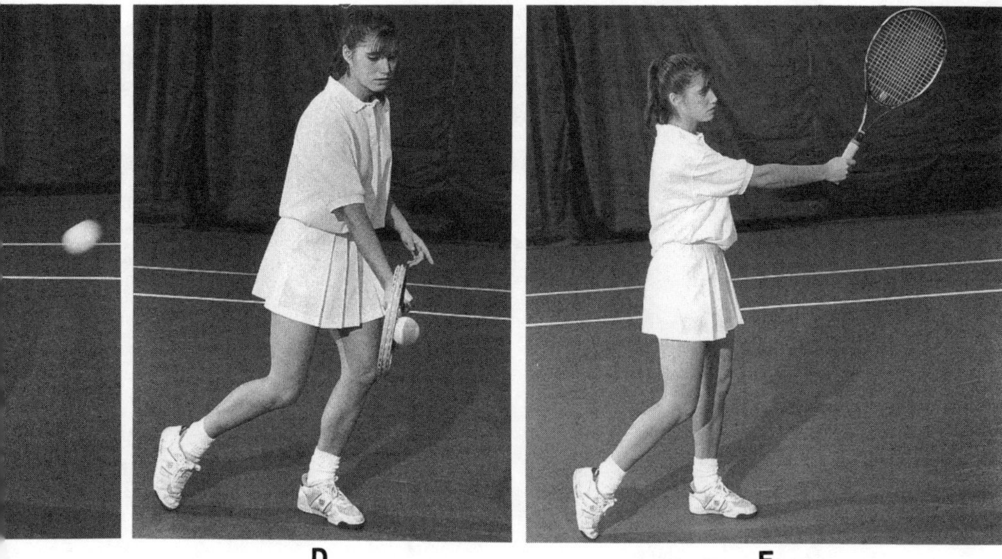

D E

above the fence on the far side of the court. Your arm is slightly bent, and you look just over your forearm. The racket face is perpendicular to the ground.

Positioning and Footwork

So far we've talked about (1) the eastern grip, (2) the waiting position with racket chest high, (3) the shoulder turn to start racket back, (4) the C-motion backswing, (5) the step into the ball, and (6) smooth contact and follow-through. You can put these six steps into practice only if you get into good position. If you stand still, the ball bounces right onto your racket about once every other year. Even if it is "right to you," you usually have to take two or three small steps. You adjust your position the way you fine-tune a radio. You move the dial boldly until you hear a sound you like, then make small adjustments until the sound is perfectly clear. If the ball is 10 feet away, turn and then take a few strides to cover ground quickly. You could get there in four large steps without "fine tuning," but you should take six or eight. As you get closer, the steps become shorter and more precise. The shoulder turn also turns your legs so you can run to the side naturally. Don't sidestep or shuffle. As you run, take the racket back gradually.

After the turn, your weight is on the right (back) foot. Ideally, you step

Jennifer Capriati makes her approach and begins the required bend for a short, low forehand. The racket position is excellent.

toward the net with the left foot before hitting. If the ball is 3 feet to your right, you could reach it in one large step. But by stepping to the side instead of into the ball, you'd lose your balance. Take two steps instead, the first with your left foot, the second with your right, stopping just to the side of the ball, your weight on the right foot. You are now balanced just as you were when you turned. Step straight toward the net with your left foot, then swing the racket forward. No matter how far you have to run, try to be stationary as you hit.

If the ball heads straight at you, turn, step backward with your right foot to clear your body from in front of the ball, and step forward with your left foot.

If you can only reach the ball on the run and can't stop and step forward with your left foot, hit the ball off the right foot. Stepping with your left foot cramps your follow-through and slows recovery to the center of the court.

Recovery

You must get back near the center of the court after hitting, but do not hurry at the expense of your balance or follow-through. Too many intermediate players rush back, worrying about the next shot before finishing this one. Let's face it: If you miss, there isn't going to be a next shot. Take your time, finish the stroke, and then get ready for another.

To get back into position, you don't just turn around and run back the way

Bjorn Borg often used an open stance on his forehand. The high follow-through is typical of heavy topspinners.

you ran to the ball, unless you're a long way out of the court. Instead, skip sideways or use crossover steps. If you turn your back on the area of the court you just came from, and that's where the return goes, you'll be slow getting to it. Keep your chest facing the net so you can move to either side with equal ease.

PLACEMENT

Cross-court shots are the staple of backcourt play, but you should first master hitting the ball straight down the line. Once you do, hitting cross court becomes simple.

To hit cross court, contact the ball a few inches farther in front than when hitting down the line. You need not make elaborate adjustments with the feet or body. If your preparation is the same for both cross-court and down-the-line shots, you have a good disguise, an essential for effective passing shots. If the stance is always the same, your opponent has no clue as to where your shots are going.

Strive to make the forehand the most powerful weapon in your game by mastering its fundamentals. Nothing can encourage your opponent more than seeing that your forehand is a chip to be exploited at will. Don't let this happen.

Boris Becker's remarkable athletic ability allows him to hit winning backhands from almost any position on the court.

3

The Backhand

There are really two backhands, the one-handed and the two-handed. Each has its advantages, but very few good players have successfully changed from one to two hands, or vice versa, except in the first few years of play.

The two-handed backhand is similar to the forehand. The left hand grips the racket with the familiar forehand grip, and the point of contact, rotation of the body, preparation, and footwork are about the same.

The main advantage of the two-handed stroke is that the extra hand gives you a great deal of leverage. It also disguises your shots because the added strength allows you to wait until the last instant before deciding where to hit. However, if you hit with two hands, you limit your reach on wide balls, and you may have trouble handling low shots as well. If you have a standard backhand volley, there's a good chance it's weak, because the two-handed ground stroke doesn't develop the strong forearm muscles needed for the one-handed volley.

There is no real disadvantage to the one-handed backhand. But to hit it well, you must develop strong forearm muscles and use a correct grip, one that gives you enough leverage.

THE ONE-HANDED BACKHAND

The one-handed backhand differs from the forehand in three major ways: Naturally the grip changes, the racket meets the ball a foot or so farther in front, and on the follow-through the body turns or rotates less.

Grip

The range of grips that work for the backhand is far narrower than for the forehand. If you hit backhands with the eastern forehand grip, the racket face is "open" (tilted upward), causing the ball to sail high off the racket. You could compensate by playing every ball with underspin, but your backhands would be strictly defensive. In addition, with this grip the palm is in front of the handle at contact, giving the racket a weak "pull" instead of a strong "push."

To find the eastern backhand grip, stand in the ready position, holding the forehand grip. Turn your shoulders to the left, rotating your hand to the left until the knuckle of the index finger is on top of the racket. The base of the thumb is firmly against the back of the racket. Place the thumb diagonally along the back of the handle or wrap it just above the middle finger. With this grip, you have the leverage to hit with force. The grip will also keep the racket face "on edge," so you won't slice unintentionally. There is some room for individuality, but if the grip is not near the eastern, you cannot create topspin without flicking your wrist over the ball, which requires great strength.

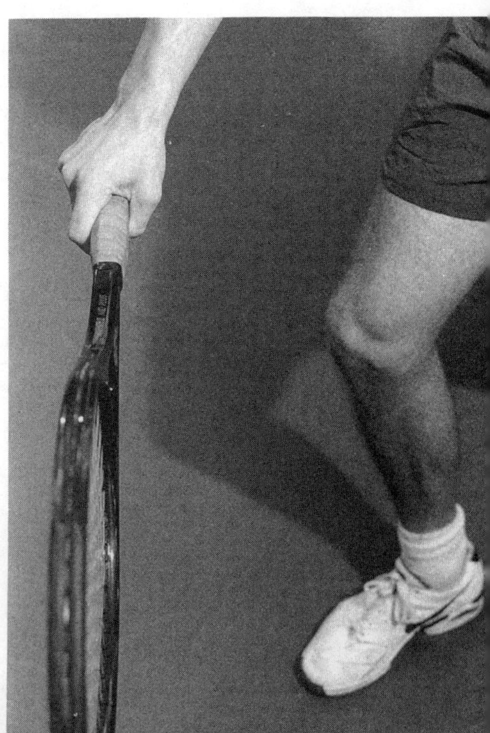

With the eastern backhand grip, the big knuckle of the index finger is on top of the racket handle. For more support, try placing the thumb diagonally along the back of the racket.

Even on hard-hit balls, it's easy to change from the forehand to the backhand grip. You must turn the shoulders anyway, and the grip change is merely part of the turn. The key is the left or free hand. This hand keeps the racket head in position while you turn, freeing the other hand to change the grip. Slow-motion films show that some top players rotate only the hand or the racket, while others rotate both. It is simpler to keep the racket face perpendicular with your left hand and do all the adjusting with your right. Use whatever works best for you, as long as the grip change is part of the entire stroke and not a separate jerk. Practice changing the grip until it is automatic. A bad grip is the number-one problem with one-handed backhands.

Turn and Backswing

The ready position is, of course, the starting point for both forehand and backhand. The instant the ball springs off your opponent's racket toward your backhand, turn your shoulders to the left and change the grip, keeping the left hand on the racket shaft. The turn points the racket to the back fence, twice as far back as it goes on the forehand turn, when it points to the side fence.

Still, the backswing on the backhand is as smooth and continuous as it is on the forehand. If time allows, you may take the racket beyond the back fence and behind your back by turning the shoulders a bit farther around. You usually won't need the extra power, because the point of contact is a foot farther in front than on the forehand, giving you more distance to accelerate the racket.

Whether you hit your backhand with one hand or two, a complete shoulder turn is essential to control the shot.

F E D

The Backhand Drive. As the ball approaches on the backhand side, the shoulders turn and the racket is carried back with the free hand (A,B). The grip change occurs during the shoulder turn. The racket continues back and under the path of the oncoming ball (C). The hit is made well in front of the body with the weight fully on the front foot (D). The arm remains straight during the follow-through (E, F).

Your backhand should be like a spring that is coiled and ready to unwind. To "coil," keep your hands close to your body on the backswing. If you hold the racket way out to the side, you will probably take it back much too high, with the result that you'll hit many balls late and won't have time to get the racket below the ball to hit topspin; to hit hard, you would have to rely on wrist action.

For rhythm and smoothness, use a C motion on the backhand as well as the forehand. However, the backhand should be a smaller C than the forehand.

Balance, Contact, Follow-through

As you turn to the left for the backhand, your weight shifts onto the left foot. Just before you start the racket forward, step toward the net with the right foot. This is a must on the backhand. On the forehand, you can often get away with hitting off the rear foot, but on the backhand, a step with the left foot makes

C B A

for a weak shot; it forces your shoulders open, sending the racket across the back of the ball instead of meeting it solidly from behind. Even if you have to step parallel to the baseline, you control the shot better by stepping with your right foot. And be sure to bend for low balls.

The point of contact should be a foot or more in front of the right hip. This is one reason you need to prepare early on the backhand: If you are the slightest bit late, your swing will be cramped and your shot weak. (If the ball gets behind you on the forehand, you can use your wrist to save it.) Many experts say that the backhand is usually the more dependable shot for good players. Obviously, this varies from player to player. It is safe to say, however, that forehands, because they are more wristy, tend to go off more often. You will master the backhand a bit more slowly, since it takes several months to develop forearm muscles strong enough to keep the racket steady when it meets a hard-hit ball. But if you establish, through practice, an early point of contact, you'll have an aggressive, effortless-looking backhand.

On the one-handed backhand, turning the hips into the shot is limited on the follow-through.

As you hit, carry the ball on the strings as long as you can and in the direction you are aiming. At contact, your body is sideways to the net. As you follow through, turn about 45 degrees so your chest faces the left net post (you open up far less than on the forehand). Your arm should be straight at contact and on the follow-through, finishing beyond your head and just past the line of flight of the ball.

On both ground strokes, check your position at the end of the follow-through. If your weight is firmly on your front foot, and the heel of your rear foot is "up" so that the bottom of your shoe faces the fence behind you, your balance and rotation are perfect.

THE TWO-HANDED BACKHAND

Grip

The added leverage you get by using the second hand enables you to hit effective two-handed backhands with almost any combination of grips. But for the basic two-handed grip, turn the right hand toward an eastern backhand grip and the left hand just above it toward an eastern forehand. Forced to play a ball (otherwise out of reach) with one hand, you can let go with the left hand and

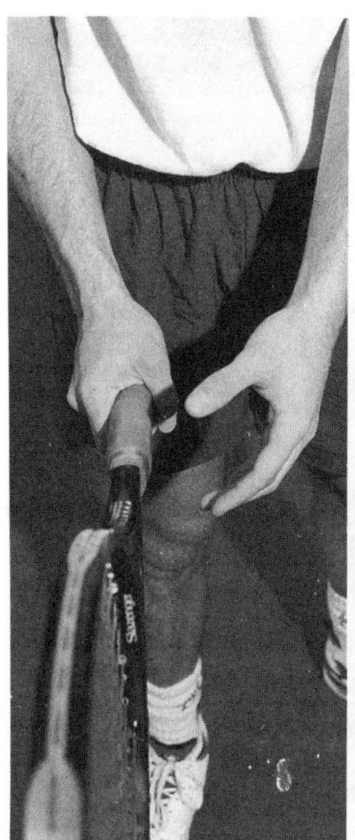

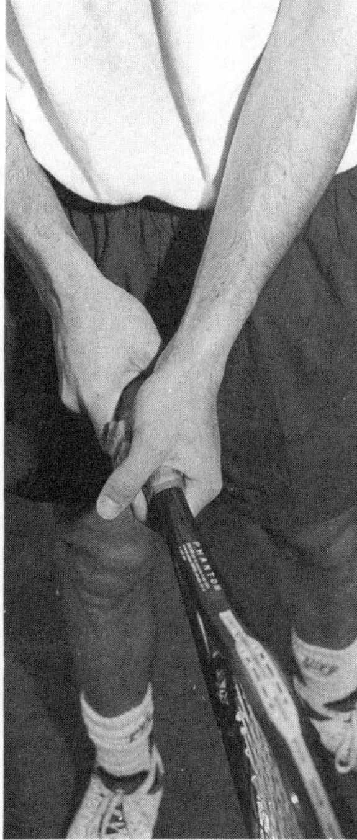

On a two-handed backhand, the left hand holds the racket with an eastern forehand grip while the grip of the right hand can vary. We recommend turning the right hand toward an eastern backhand grip.

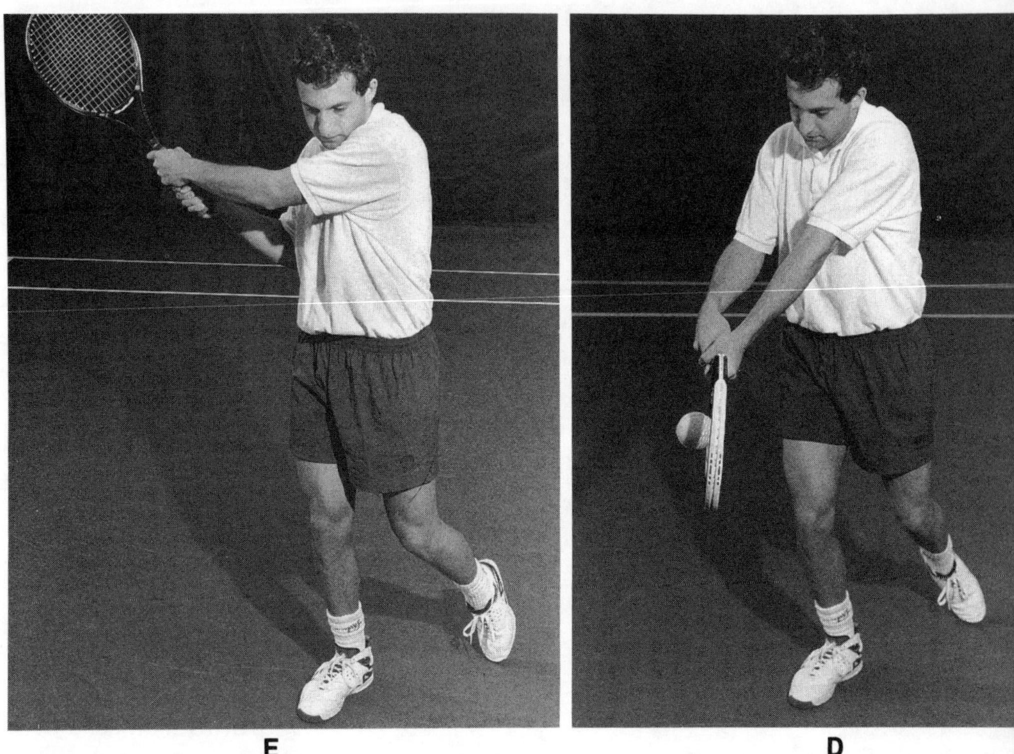

E D

The Two-Handed Backhand. The shoulder turn resembles that of the one-handed backhand (A, B), but on the backswing the left arm is bent while the right arm is relatively straight (C). The point of contact is just in front of the right hip (D). The follow-through is similar to that of a left-handed forehand, with the hips and shoulders turned toward the net (E).

hit a one-handed backhand with a proper grip. The grip also gives you a stable two-handed stroke. And the better you acquaint yourself with a continental or eastern backhand grip, the easier it is to master the one-handed backhand volley.

Backswing and Contact

The backswing should still be a C motion. You generate enough power without it, but the C allows you to hit topspin, slice, or drop shots with the same

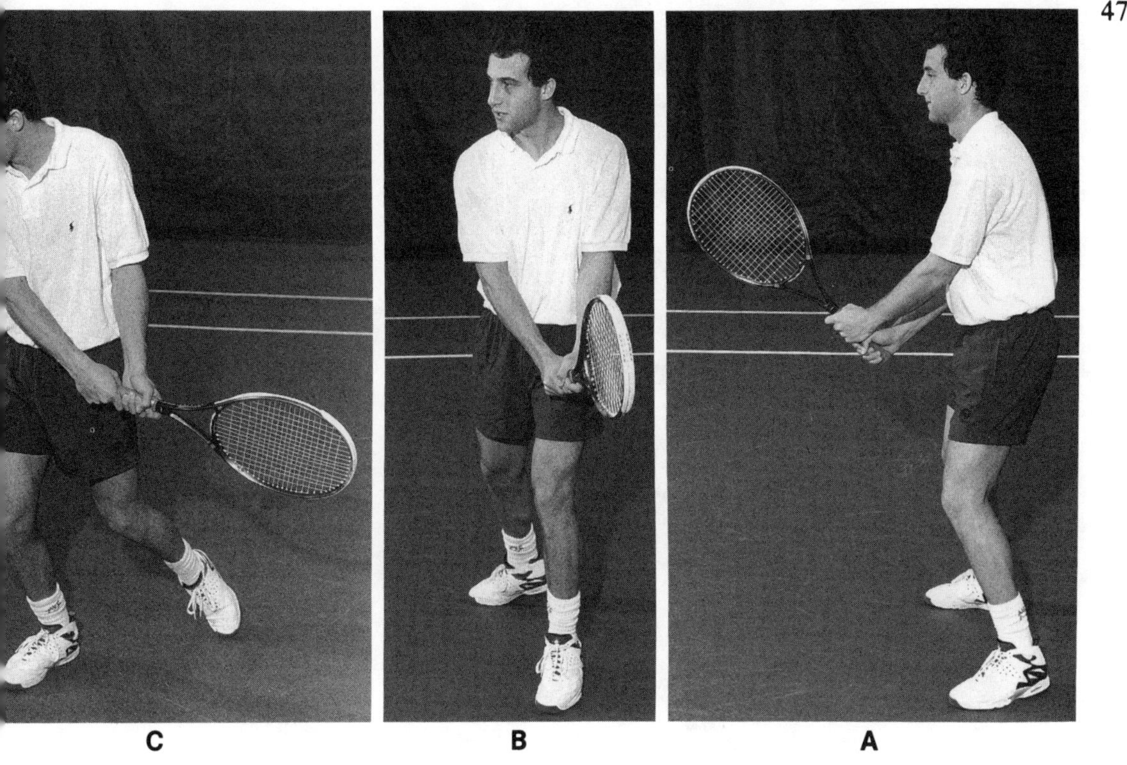

C B A

preparation. If you take the racket directly below the level of the ball, it will be difficult to slice and disguise your shots.

Once again, "coil" to produce power and topspin by keeping your hands close to your body. You have to get closer to the ball to hit effectively with two hands anyway.

Your point of contact is the same as on the forehand. If you hit the ball too far in front, you will have to twist around to keep the swing smooth. If you are a bit late, the extra hand on the racket can be a real lifesaver. The added strength produces good shots in almost hopeless situations.

Perfect concentration and balance on the two-handed back hand. Note that the grip of former tennis star Chris Evert combines the continental for the right hand and the eastern forehand for the left.

Topspin

It is often easier to hit topspin with the two-handed grip. Many players push down with the right hand and pull up with the left as they swing forward, to accentuate the low-to-high motion needed to hit topspin. If you want to hit flat or with slight topspin, keep the right arm fairly straight from the end of the backswing through the point of contact.

Follow through as you would on a left-handed forehand. Turn your hips in toward the net and keep your left arm fairly straight. After hitting through the ball, let both arms bend a bit, allowing the racket to fly through naturally. The left arm bends only when the ball is long gone. The weight should be balanced on the front foot; once again, if the heel of the rear foot is "up," you have shifted your weight properly.

Many top players use underspin for added control on their backhands. Note the open racket face in this slice by Jana Novotna.

Underspin Backhands

Sooner or later, most players find it necessary or advantageous to slice the ball. If the ball gets behind your contact point for topspin, your only choice is a slice. Your slice will often give your opponent fits. It is tailor made for approach shots or counterpunching off a forcing ground stroke.

The slice is simple to hit. You may take your regular C backswing, but hold the racket above the level of the approaching ball. If you keep the racket face perpendicular to the ground, you will drive the ball straight into the court. Therefore, keep the racket face open throughout the swing. A full follow-through is essential for good control.

The Serve

Top players, from the junior through the professional ranks, dazzle spectators with the force of their serves. The fastest men's serves travel at over 130 miles per hour, the fastest women's at over 100. But even at a Wimbledon or a U.S. Open, serves hit with such blinding speed are not needed to win.

Most of us have neither the size and strength nor the time to develop a consistent, high-speed serve and must settle for a dependable, effective one instead. The serve can be the most devastating weapon in your arsenal, but the first priority is to keep it from being your Achilles' heel.

DEVELOPING AN EFFECTIVE SERVE

To develop an effective serve, keep these points in mind as you practice: (1) Get the ball in the box, (2) place the ball, (3) hit for depth, and (4) add spin and power.

Accuracy

Accuracy is perhaps the most crucial part of good serving. The beginner has placed the ball well if it

As Steffi Graf demonstrates, good form and perfect timing are the requisites of an effective serve.

lands in the correct service court. The intermediate player succeeds if the ball is directed to the opponent's forehand or backhand. The advanced player is more ambitious still, attempting to keep the opponent guessing and off balance by varying not only placement but speed and spin as well.

From their first day on the court, many players make the mistake of blasting the first serve. Their confidence wanes when only a few balls go in, and they resort to a harmless push on the second serve that begs to be pounced upon. If your first serve misses regularly, your serving game is only as effective as your second serve. This is as true for world-class players as for public-park hackers. An accurate second serve, then, is the foundation of good serving.

Placement

As a beginner, you must get the second serve in the square every time. When your second serve becomes reliable, experiment a bit with the first serve. But don't stand there and try to knock the fuzz off the ball. Blasting the first serve hinders development of one consistent motion, because the two serves are so vastly different in feeling. Your second serve will lag behind the first. Develop both serves simultaneously. On the first serve, try placing the ball. See if you can direct it to the opponent's backhand. By hitting close to the corners, you create openings where you can place your next shot.

Depth

The depth on both first and second serves is as important as the direction. A short serve invites the other player to step into the ball and take control of the point, while a deep serve, even if medium speed, keeps your opponent pinned to the baseline. As the depth of your serve improves, its speed increases naturally. Top players try to keep the ball within a foot or so of the service line.

Spin and Power

Once your serve is consistent and fairly deep, add spin. By varying spin, you can alter the bounce of the ball, keeping your opponent off balance. The technique for changing spins is explained later in this chapter. But most important, spin gives the server more margin for error over the net. As on the ground strokes, a bit of topspin (or a combination of topspin and sidespin) makes the ball dip quickly after it crosses the net. Spin, therefore, gives you the security to hit the ball hard—and several feet over the net. The height and speed combine to produce depth. Booming flat serves tend to be erratic because they must skim the net to go in. Every top player serves with some spin for control.

HOW TO SERVE

Grip and Stance

As you improve, your service grip may go through a series of changes. Most beginners feel awkward and lose control when serving with the continental or eastern backhand grips used by most top players. With the continental, the ball often spins off weakly to one side of the court. If so, start with an eastern forehand grip. Avoid the western grip at all costs, although it may be the easiest way to get the ball in the court. It is essentially a "no progress" grip that is difficult to change once you are used to it. The eastern forehand grip, however, gives you the control you need at the beginning and requires a less dramatic change when you are ready to add spin.

In the service stance, your body is sideways to the net, allowing your hips and shoulders to turn and transfer your weight as you hit. Standing sideways, hold the racket shaft with the fingertips of the left hand so that the racket head is just above your waist and points toward the net. (Yes, there is room to hold a ball or two and still support the racket.) Relax your right arm and squeeze the racket just enough to keep it from flopping around or twisting in your hand. Position your feet about shoulder width apart. Place the right or back foot parallel to the baseline and the left foot a couple of inches behind the baseline, with the toe pointing toward the net post to your right. Keep your body weight on your back foot. Some good players start with the weight forward, rocking back as they begin, but shifting the weight twice complicates things for inexperienced players.

Backswing

To start the motion, move the hands in unison in a "down together, up together" pattern. The left hand drops down to prepare to toss the ball and the right takes the racket back into the hitting position. Move the hands slowly. The racket obviously cannot begin moving toward the ball until the left hand tosses it.

The left hand goes down to a point a few inches from the left thigh and sweeps upward without a hitch to start the toss. Keep the arm straight as it

A

B

C

The Serve. Begin with the free hand either touching or cradling the racket (A). The arms separate (B) and move smoothly into the backswing and toss (C). The racket drops into its power loop (D) and accelerates into the point of contact (E). A full follow-through adds to the pace of the serve (F).

rises. Avoid jerking the fingers or wrist. Lift the arm smoothly, releasing the ball when the arm is fully extended to a point just above the head. Don't heave the ball—toss it no higher than your outstretched racket. Contact the ball about one foot in front of you and slightly to the right of your head. Some good players vary the toss slightly, depending on the type of serve they are hitting, but the more uniform your toss, the harder it is for the receiver to "read" what is coming.

While the left hand puts the ball into position to hit, the right hand carries the racket back. The racket moves in a pendulum arc, dropping down and then rising toward the fence behind you. If you relax, the racket opens naturally, allowing your arm to move smoothly. The timing is correct if your right arm

D E F

is roughly parallel to the ground when the left hand releases the ball. This position marks the end of the backswing.

Power Loop

The "power loop" follows the backswing. The term refers to the path of the racket head as it loops and accelerates behind your back. The backswing has been slow, but now the racket head is ready to pick up speed. From the end of the backswing, simply bend your elbow to drop the racket head, which then travels over your head, past your left shoulder, down to your waist, and finally

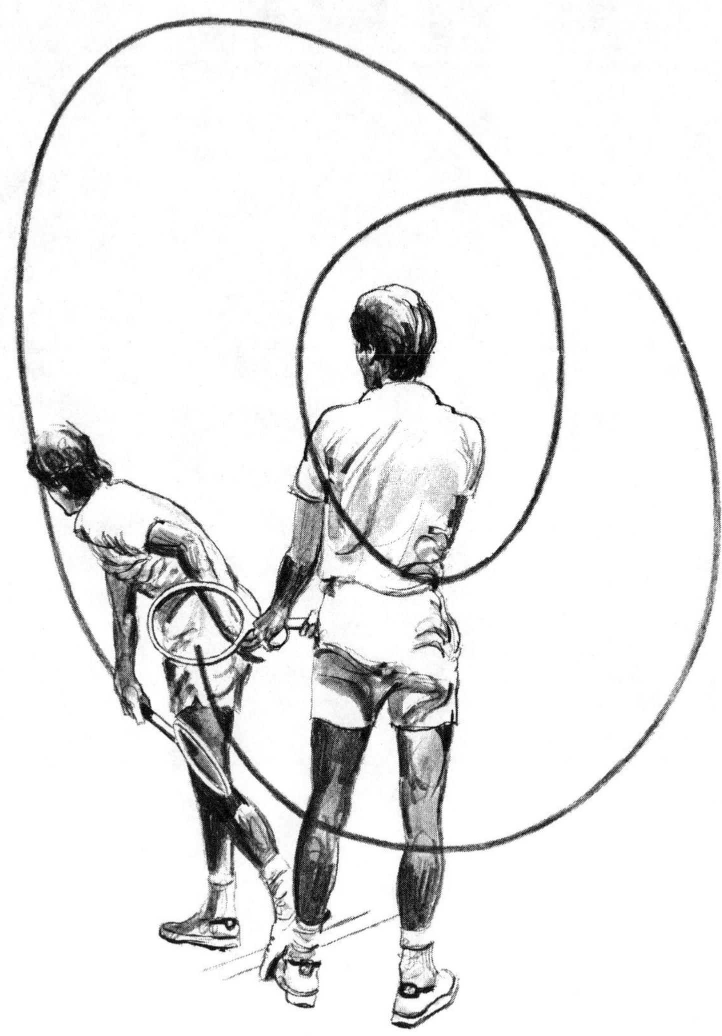

Power Loop. On the serve, the racket essentially follows a circular path with a loop at the top. It is essential that this loop be continuous.

—as your elbow comes forward and the arm straightens—up to meet the ball. When you drop the racket, the hitting side faces your back. The entire loop takes only a fraction of a second.

Most of the pitfalls in serving occur during this looping or "backscratching" motion. If you do not complete the loop, you rob yourself of power. If you stop the loop at any point, you lose the momentum you've accumulated. But

Despite individual mannerisms, all good servers have a power loop. Here we see its beginning.

the biggest mistake is failing to drop the racket behind the back at all. Like many players, you may fear that you can't make the loop and still have time to hit the ball, so you stop the racket above your right shoulder and wait for the ball to descend. Drop the racket; you have plenty of time.

Ideally, as the racket head rises to meet the ball, the edge, as opposed to the face, approaches the ball. To hit a flat serve, turn the face into the ball just before the hit by rotating the hand. To hit a spin serve, angle the racket slightly at contact and alter the path of the swing. The same principle applies to the ground strokes. You will probably find it easiest to learn a relatively flat serve first, because the ball travels exactly where the face of the racket is pointing at contact. On the other hand, it takes time to learn both to spin the ball *and* to hit it where you aim.

A good demonstration of shoulder rotation on the serve. Note the eyes glued to the ball.

Power servers tend to toss the ball well out in front in order to lean into the ball for added leverage.

Follow-through

The follow-through, like the backswing, is semicircular. After contact, the racket continues in a full arc, passing the left side of the body. For added power, step into the court with the right foot.

Good servers, of course, add some sophisticated touches to the basic motion. For example, most of them bend the knees and arch the back a bit. If you don't do these things naturally from the beginning, don't try them until your motion is sound and your serve consistent. Such movements give good serves a more athletic or graceful appearance, but they detract from the efficiency of the swing if not smoothly integrated into the motion.

Your goal is to keep the service motion continuous and economical. A pause, hitch, or flourish may be costly.

CORRECTING ERRORS

If your basic motion is sound, you should be able to recognize and correct errors in your serve as you practice or play.

We generally make errors in patterns. You may leave the court declaring that 90 percent of your serves were long that day. If you are alert enough to see that you are hitting long, you should be able to do something about it.

You can trace many problems to your toss. If the ball is going consistently long, you are probably tossing too far behind you so that, at contact, the racket face points up toward the sky rather than toward your target, the service box. Tossing a bit forward into the court gives your serve a lower arc.

If you net the ball consistently, you probably toss too far in front of you. The racket head comes down as it meets the ball, driving it into the net.

A very low toss may cause the ball to go either long or short. It goes long if the racket face gets under the ball (the way you'd hit a pop fly in baseball). It lands short if you flick your racket down over the ball. The ideal toss is about as high as your outstretched racket, giving you time to complete the power loop and the follow-through.

If your serve is erratic but there is no pattern to your errors, your toss may be moving around too much, preventing you from developing the serving rhythm that is the key to consistency. To improve the toss, hit practice serves while trying to keep the right foot stationary. The toss must be in the right place if you are to hit, because you can't chase it. Let the heel come up, allowing the

On the flat serve, the contact point is directly behind the ball. On the slice serve, the racket brushes the right side of the ball. On the topspin serve, the racket makes contact on the upper right-hand side.

body weight to shift forward, but don't take a step. If you find this drill difficult at first, you may discover that you've been moving the foot more to adjust for bad tosses than to add power.

Watch the ball carefully. If you mis-hit regularly, especially into the net, you may be pulling your head down just before contact, perhaps because you're overanxious to see where the serve is going. Hit a few practice serves, leaving your head up until you hear the ball hit on the other side of the net. Your mis-hit problem should disappear.

ADDING SPIN

If your service motion is fairly well grooved and you feel confident that the ball will go in if you hit it at moderate speeds, you should add spin to the ball.

The slice is the easiest spin serve to learn. You might be able to hit a slice on your first attempt simply by changing your grip farther toward the backhand. With this small adjustment, the racket face contacts the ball at a slight angle, usually directing the first few dozen serves much lower than your flat serve and farther to the left. This is exactly what should happen. The trick is to alter your aim, directing the ball higher and farther to the right than usual. Your serves will gradually zero in on the correct service box as your grip becomes more comfortable, ending the need to overcompensate.

If you already use the continental or backhand service grip, visualize the ball as the face of a clock. On a flat serve, you contact the ball in the center of the clock. On the slice serve, you hit it on the right side, at 3 o'clock. Although slow-motion studies show little change in where the racket contacts the ball on the various serves, the server can definitely feel a difference. As on the ground strokes, you direct the ball by hitting with the racket face at the angle you want, and you choose the type of spin by adjusting the racket's path.

You may find the slice easier to learn—and to put more spin on—by tossing out to your right. But for disguise, try to keep your tosses uniform.

The slice serve tends to stay low and skid along the court. Moving like a curve ball in baseball, it shoots out to the server's left. It works best when hit to a right-hander's forehand, a lefty's backhand, or right at the receiver, where it cramps the return.

The classical American twist serve bounces sharply to the server's right. The American twist has its shortcomings. Since the toss is far to the left, you must arch your back to hit it, which is tiring and makes the spin and direction easy for your opponent to anticipate. And the ball moves slowly. More valuable is the topspin serve, a combination of twist and slice. It has many advantages: (1) the ball clears the net by a wide margin, (2) the ball jumps forward after the bounce, and (3) you hit the serve with essentially the same toss you use on a flat or slice serve. On the topspin serve, the racket meets the top right part of the ball, or at roughly 1:30 on the clock.

Good players use some spin on most first serves and all second serves. Decide what is comfortable and reliable for you, and mix your speeds and spins wisely, the way a pitcher varies his delivery.

To practice serving, divide both service courts into three lanes, the two outside lanes for wide serves and the middle one for serves aimed right at the receiver. Hit three different serves (flat, slice, or topspin) into each lane, then vary the speeds. Use your head, use spin, and practice. You don't need a great deal of strength to serve effectively.

Quickness, concentration, and endless practice made Billie Jean King one of the best volleyers in tennis history.

5

Volley and Overhead

A volley is any ball hit before it bounces. Hitting a volley, or volleying, is the basic shot in playing net and is perhaps the easiest stroke to learn. Unfortunately, it is also the most difficult one to execute in play. You have about half the time to react to an oncoming ball when standing at the net as you do when positioned behind the baseline. You must anticipate where the ball is going to come from, prepare early, and move quickly. If you get to the ball, it is easy to hit because the stroke is so simple.

Net play is often taboo for inexperienced players. But shortly after you begin playing, make the volley an integral part of your game. Otherwise, your matches will proceed like chess stalemates. You may be able to maneuver your opponents beautifully, but you won't be able to finish them off.

PLAYING NET

Fear is the downfall of most net players—fear that they will be passed or lobbed over, fear that they will miss the shot. Overcome these fears. Those who can maneuver an opponent, create an open-

Forehand Volley. From the ready position (A), the first priority is to place the racket face in the path of the oncoming ball (B). The point of contact is well in front of the body (C) and the follow-through is compact (D).

ing, and pop a volley into the open court know the thrill of controlling a point. Without these skills, the game is largely a matter of waiting for your opponent to miss or being victimized by an opponent who can volley. Even if you have terrific ground strokes, you must be able to attack the net when granted an opening.

For everyone but the experienced player, the thought of being hit, especially in doubles, by an overhead ball at close range is the scariest part of playing net. If you feel your life is in danger, get out of the way, although in most cases you can defend yourself with your racket much quicker than by ducking. Your best defense, however, is to stay alert and sharpen your reflexes through practice.

The fear of losing points at the net through your opponent's winners or your own errors vanishes as you gain volleying experience. Many youngsters who succeed with a defensive, error-free style never improve and eventually lose interest in the game because they can't make the transition to the controlled but attacking style needed to beat mature players. In the end, defensive players play to avoid losing, while offensive players, who attack the net, play to win.

C D

HOW TO VOLLEY

There are three fundamentals of volleying: (1) Take a short backswing, (2) keep the racket head and your eyes as close as possible to the level of the ball, and (3) hit the ball in front of you.

1. On most volleys, there just isn't time to take a full swing. Use a short backswing to line up the racket quickly behind the ball.

2. The closer your eyes are to the level of the ball, the more clearly you will see it. On low shots, you must bend down to control the racket head. If you stand up straight, your wrist loosens, your racket head drops, and your volley turns into a weak slap.

3. As the ball approaches, reach out to hit it in front, while you have it clearly in view. If you wait until the ball reaches your side, you will have to jerk your head to follow it, and if you see the point of contact at all, it is apt to be out of focus. In addition, by volleying the ball in front, you can put your body weight behind the shot.

Grips

If you use the continental grip, the racket face naturally opens a bit on both sides. This advantage, and the time saved by playing both forehand and backhand volleys without changing grips, makes the continental the choice of most accomplished volleyers. However, a few advanced players—and most novices—prefer the added support provided by the eastern grip. Whichever you choose, the fundamentals of volleying are the same.

Distance from the Net

At first glance, it would seem that the best place to stand for a volley is very close to the net; from there, you could angle your volleys sharply and escape playing tough low shots. At times, good players do virtually hang over the net. But be practical. Any opponent spotting you so close will naturally pop the ball over your head. Your aggressiveness may backfire, and you'll spend more time chasing lobs than hitting volleys. A good starting point is about the middle of the 21-foot service court, halfway between the service line and the net. From this position, take a few steps forward, called "closing," and you're on top of the net for an occasional kill.

Positioning the Racket

If the ball is coming to your forehand while you're at net in the ready position, first bend the wrist a bit to the right to put the racket head in the path of the ball. Then, if you have time, turn your shoulders slightly to the right as well. This turn gives you all the backswing you need. Don't make the fatal error of pulling back your elbow—and the racket along with it. Keep your elbow in front of your body. If the ball is approaching fast, just meet it squarely, with a firm grip, to send it back with good pace. On slower balls, turn your shoulders to add the little backswing needed to generate some power. But never take the racket back beyond your head. To put away high floaters, some good players hit drive volleys, which resemble forehand ground strokes, but that takes years of experience to perfect.

Footwork and Timing

Once you've mastered the stroke, work on your footwork and timing. You can generate remarkable pace with a tiny backswing. The key is to step forward and

Getting down on low volleys is crucial (above). Moving wide for a volley (right), Martina Navratilova shows how the free arm is used for balance.

lean in. Just before hitting, step with your left foot across your right and toward the net. The timing of the step is crucial. Stepping too early commits your weight before the ball arrives and throws you off balance. For the best possible timing, plant the left foot a fraction of a second before contact, so when you meet the ball your feet are stable and your body leans forward.

The Forehand Volley

Hit your volleys with a bit of underspin for control. Completely flat volleys often sail out. To hit underspin, open the racket face at least a little on all volleys. On low volleys, you have a second reason to open the face: to lift the ball up. The lower the volley, the more you have to open. But even on balls shoulder high or above, when a flat volley would work fairly well, most good players open the face slightly for underspin to give the ball a low, skidding bounce. On high volleys, start the racket above the level of the ball and hit slightly down and through it. But don't slice or hack at the ball. Keep the wrist firm at contact to avoid hitting excessive underspin.

The key to effective volleying is a firm wrist at the point of contact, even when lunging for a wide ball as Boris Becker does here.

To find the point of contact for a forehand volley, stand sideways to a mirror, holding the slightly open racket face in front of you and pointing the racket butt to your left knee. Pointing the butt lifts the racket head above your wrist, where it is held firmly, a key to crisp volleying. On the backhand volley, place the racket diagonally across your body so the butt points to the right knee.

At contact, your wrist should be firm and your arm slightly bent. The ball travels in the direction your racket face points at contact. To aim the ball cross court or down the line, adjust the face *before* the hit. Attempting to change your aim during contact usually causes a wristy error.

The follow-through is brief but important. After contact, keep the racket face moving a foot or so in the direction you are hitting. A sudden stop causes the ball to fly wildly off the racket, while a ground-strokelike follow-through results in wristy, erratic volleys. Good volleys tend to be compact and crisp.

The Backhand Volley

The backhand volley's fundamentals—shoulder turn, footwork, and follow-through—are the same as the forehand's. Once again, the first priority is to put the racket face in the path of the ball. There is, however, one difference between the two volleys: At contact on the backhand, the arm is straight but not stiff.

VOLLEYS REQUIRING UNUSUAL FOOTWORK

If the ball is coming right at you, you must learn not only to defend yourself from getting hit but to hit an effective return as well. If the ball is below your shoulder, use a backhand volley. Backhand volleys shield you against the hardest-hit balls and even allow you to return them comfortably, if not aggressively. Simply pull the racket over to block balls as far to the right as your right hip. Hitting these shots with the forehand volley cramps you, causing mis-hits.

If the ball is above your shoulder, it is usually traveling slowly if it is going to stay in the court. You have plenty of time, so lean to the left, or step left with your left foot, and play the ball as a forehand.

When you are forced to move wide, the footwork on the volley is very different from that on the ground strokes, where you have time to take some large steps, then fine-tune your position with some small ones. On the volley, you're in more of a hurry, so you must learn to cover half the court in two steps. To reach a wide forehand volley, push off with your left foot, sidestep with your right, cross over with your left, and hit. To get to a wide backhand volley, push

D C B

off with the right foot, land on the left, step across with the right, and hit. Although tall players often seem unpassable at the net because of their tremendous reach, quick, well-trained small players often handle wide balls just as well.

VARIATIONS OF THE VOLLEY

The Drive Volley

Sometimes, good players take a full swing at a volley. When most of us try these drive volleys, they fly out of control. So it is best to use them sparingly or not at all.

The Drop Volley

A drop volley, however, is easier to execute and is often your best option. If your opponent is standing well behind the baseline, tapping the ball just over the net may win the point more easily than hitting it hard. Drop volleys are especially effective against low, slow-moving shots. To hit a drop volley, eliminate all backswing and, at contact, open or "slide" the racket face under the ball. Also loosen the grip slightly to let your wrist, rather than your racket, absorb the shock of the ball and prevent it from rebounding deep into the court. If your opponent is in good position, a drop volley is too risky; just block the ball into the open court.

A

On a backhand volley, use the face hand to position the racket (A, B). As with the forehand volley, the point of contact is in front of the body (C) and the follow-through is compact (D).

To volley a ball coming directly at you, use a backhand.

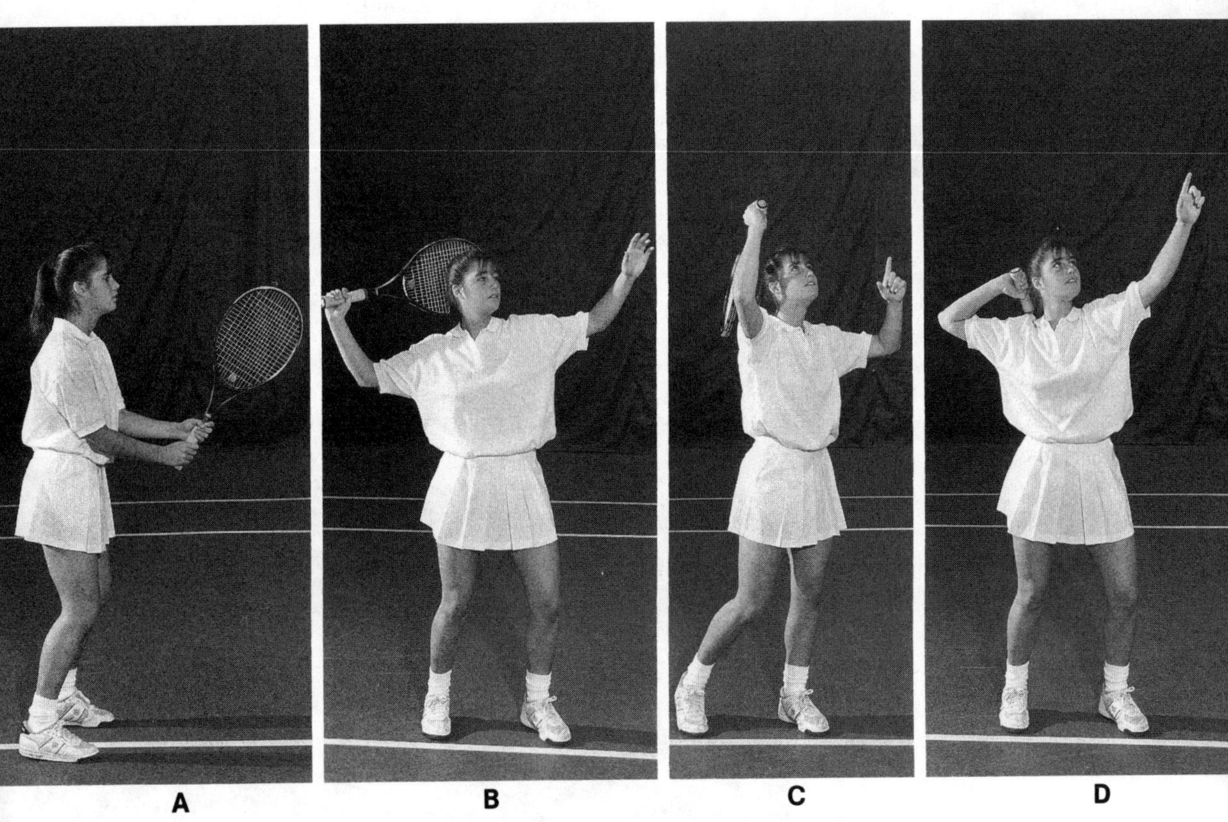

Overhead. From the ready position (A), the initial movement on the overhead smash is to get the shoulders sideways to the net, then raise the racket to a position back behind the body (B) and begin a power loop similar to that of the serving motion (C, D). The arm is fully extended on contact (E) and the follow-through is full (F, G).

The Two-Handed Volley

Two-handed volleys have serious limitations. They restrict your reach on wide balls, and they are awkward on shots that come right at you. If your basic volley is two-handed, it helps to develop a one-handed stroke to volley these difficult shots. The fundamentals are the same on the one- and two-handed volleys.

E F G

THE OVERHEAD

The overhead smash resembles the serve—the grip, the forward swing, and the follow-through are essentially the same—but it is at once easier and more difficult. It is easier because you can place an overhead anywhere in your opponent's court, not just in the service box, and because you hit it from inside the baseline, which lets you angle the ball more sharply. The overhead smash is more difficult because you must hit your opponent's lob, which is intended to throw you off balance, rather than your own toss, and because high lobs are often difficult to judge since they descend quickly.

If you make the proper move to take the racket back the instant you spot an overhead, you're bound to have a consistent smash. First, turn your shoulders to the right and step back with the right foot; you are now sideways, ready to sidestep back for deep balls. Then point the left arm in the direction of the ball and draw the racket back with the right. The left arm keeps you sideways to the net, and on balance, and acts as a pointer that helps you sight the ball. For rhythm and power, first take the racket back behind your head; then, just before the hit, drop it behind your back. If you take it all the way back at the start, you will have to stop it there while you wait for the ball to drop.

If you're hitting the ball on the fly, keep your feet moving to get in the best possible position and then stop, take one step forward with the left foot, and hit. Players who plant their feet too early often misjudge the ball. Players with good overheads seem to "dance" until the ball is about 10 feet above them; then they step and hit.

If the lob is deep, you may be forced to jump for the ball. The jumping

To smash a deep lob, you may be forced to leap for the ball with a classic scissors kick (right) . . . or with a desperate, not-so-classic reach (far right).

action is called a "scissors kick." As you move backward, push off the ground with the right foot, kick that foot forward to stay on balance, and land on the left foot.

Most overheads carry very little spin. As in the flat serve, turn the racket face flat against the ball with the wrist. When you are returning an extremely high and deep lob after the bounce, however, take a fuller backswing and lead with the racket edge to add spin for control.

You should neither push an overhead nor try to rip the cover off the ball. If you hit softly, your opponent will sense your lack of confidence; if you pound the ball, you will usually drop your head before contact and mis-hit. Steady, well-placed overheads with medium pace make your opponent think twice before lobbing again.

Learn to move to your left to cut off lobs headed for your backhand. Very few players can smash effectively on the backhand side. If you are forced to play a backhand overhead, hit it as you would a high volley and hustle into position for the next shot.

Because the ball falls rapidly, the smash requires precise timing. To improve your timing, practice hitting overheads every time you warm up. A good smash is the cornerstone of your net game.

Defensive lobs when you are hopelessly out of position can often get you back into the point.

Special Ground Strokes

When we think of ground strokes, we usually visualize two players stroking the ball back and forth from the baselines. Although these shots are the bread and butter of your ground game, six other strokes—the return of serve, the approach shot, the half-volley, the passing shot, the lob, and the drop shot—are technically ground strokes but have specialized swings or uses that set them apart from standard forehands and backhands.

THE RETURN OF SERVE

You should use one swing when returning a soft serve, another when facing a hard or heavy spin delivery. Against a weak serve, hit the return with an ordinary forehand or backhand stroke by turning your shoulders and then taking a good-sized backswing. When facing a hard serve, however, simply turn your shoulders and hit. This abbreviated backswing produces returns that are consistent and crisp, because the hard-hit ball rebounds off your racket with pace. Against the average player, who usually hits medium-paced serves but occasionally throws in a fast or slow one, turn your shoulders, adjust your feet, and

When waiting to return a serve, be on your toes, ready to move forward into the ball.

consider it a luxury if you have time to take a full swing. Be careful. You may have less time than you think. A short backswing is always safe, a long one is not. As on the volley, a large backswing may cause late hits.

Regardless of the speed of the serve, turn as soon as you can see which side the ball is coming to. To check if your turn is quick enough, freeze your position at the instant one of your opponent's service faults hits the net. If your shoulders are sideways and your feet are ready to step into the ball, you're turning on time to hit back the hardest serves. If not, watch your opponent's toss and contact point more carefully, to pick up the serve's direction, and turn that way the instant after the hit.

Make your footwork as quick and economical as your backswing. While waiting for the serve, lean slightly forward on the balls of your feet rather than sitting back on your heels. Reaction time is often slowed by tension, so relax your shoulders and knees and be ready to spring to either side. Just before your opponent contacts the ball, make a small "ready hop" to get a quick start.

Above all, don't back away from the ball. You'll miss the return or pop

Andre Agassi and the late great Arthur Ashe, playing shoulder-high service returns. You must get the shoulders sideways to the net even if there is little time to move the feet.

it up in the air. You may have to stand several feet behind the baseline to gain enough time to step forward to meet a hard serve, but once you decide on a position, hold your ground.

Another cause of weak returns is straightening your knees or jumping into the air as you hit. Keep the knees bent and the body stable. Staying down guides your racket along a fairly level plane toward the approaching ball. Any jerk of the body causes a loss of control. You must be on balance, of course, to counteract the force of the serve.

Try to follow through. By keeping the ball on the strings, you drive the shot. Against a very hard serve, players often block the ball and make the mistake of stopping the racket at the point of contact, which results in hitting a high floater. A short follow-through will eliminate this tendency.

The type of spin you use on the return is not very important. You simply don't have time to take the big swing needed to hit heavy topspin. Since most serves bounce fairly high, the returns are hit from around shoulder level, a point well above the top of the net. Against an opponent who rushes net on the serve, however, you need topspin or underspin to keep the ball low. Using a short backswing, either hit up slightly (to generate topspin) or chip, which produces underspin and takes the speed off the serve. Either shot puts the ball at your opponent's feet, forcing a half-volley or a weak volley up in return.

Once you're able to get the ball back consistently, try to make your return a weapon. A few winning returns damages the confidence of the server, who strains to hit better and better serves and hits more faults instead.

Against heavy spin serves, move in to cut the ball off as it rises. These serves swing wide as they bounce, pulling you out of the court if you don't attack them. Twist serves, moreover, often bounce high, so intercept the ball before it kicks over your shoulder.

THE APPROACH SHOT

An approach shot is an attacking stroke hit from midcourt that allows you to move to the net. In a baseline rally, both players are content to keep the ball in play until one of them hits short (to around the service line). Then the other player moves in to hit an approach shot, and things begin to happen. The point will end in short order, usually in favor of the net rusher—if the approach shot was good.

The approach shot is not an end in itself but a means to get in position to win the point with a volley. It is similar to the shot a golfer hits to approach the green. The golfer's aim is to set up an easy putt; if the ball happens to go in the hole, it's a bonus. The same is true in tennis: You should expect the ball to come back. If it doesn't, so much the better. Don't take unnecessary chances on short balls. You're on the offensive, so it's unfortunate to give the point away with a careless error. Put the pressure on your opponent to perform.

Approach shots are hit like other ground strokes, with two exceptions. Since you are closer to the net, reduce the size of your backswing to hit the shorter distance. And you're moving forward, so stop for an instant to hit. Be careful, because the forward motion puts extra weight into your shot, which may cause you to over-hit.

Use the spin you feel most comfortable with. Many accomplished players use underspin to make the ball skid as it bounces and then stay low, forcing

Top players tend to rotate the shoulders as they run forward to play approach shots.

the opponent to hit the passing shot up, where it is easy to put away on the volley. Experiment with the slice approach first, and if it doesn't work, try topspin and flat shots, choosing the more natural of the two. As usual, depth is all-important. It's better to hit a deep, forcing topspin approach than a short, feeble slice.

In most cases, hit approach shots down the line to put yourself in the best position to reach your opponent's passing shots. But make an exception when you can exploit a very weak stroke by hitting cross court. The strategy involved in placing approach shots is explained in Chapter 9.

Not all short balls, of course, call for an approach shot. If you catch the ball very short and high, simply clobber it for a winner.

THE HALF-VOLLEY

The half-volley is played just after the bounce, while the ball is still rising. It is similar to the short-hop balls played by baseball infielders.

You hit most half-volleys in serve and volley play or after an approach shot, when you're moving through the middle of the court on your way to the net and the ball lands at your feet. Since the half-volley is hard to time because the ball is rising, move in whenever possible to take the ball before the bounce. But when forced to half-volley, do it offensively and you'll be a much better net rusher, especially in serve-and-volley play.

Despite its name, a half-volley is hit more like an abbreviated ground stroke than a volley. On a low volley, you open the racket face; on a half-volley, you keep the racket face perpendicular to the court.

The fundamentals for forehand and backhand half-volleys are:

- Get down to the ball. If you don't bend the knees, you will invariably pop the ball up in the air.
- Use a short, compact backswing.
- Use a firm wrist, keep the racket on edge, and watch the ball closely.
- Stay down and follow through.

A

B

Perfect form for the half-volley: body low, weight balanced, racquet forward to meet the ball early.

C

The half-volley. Bring your racket to the side the ball is coming toward (A). Staying down and meeting the ball early are essential ingredients (B). Try to stay down throughout the follow-through (C).

THE PASSING SHOT

Unlike other ground-stroke variations, the passing shot is hit with the same stroke as the regular baseline ground stroke. Both, moreover, require patience. Don't panic when your opponent is at the net; you may need two or more shots to move him or her around enough to create the opening for a passing shot. However, there are two elements that, while important on the regular ground strokes, are critical on passing shots: disguise and topspin.

The key to disguise is early and uniform preparation. If you set up for each shot quickly, presenting the same picture, your opponent will have trouble reading where you're aiming your passing shots. If you set your feet each time as if to hit down the line, you simply meet the ball a few inches farther in front of you to pull it sharply cross court. Learn to hit in either direction from one stance. Just before you hit, concentrate on the ball, but be aware of your opponent's position on the court.

The second necessity on passing shots is topspin. It makes the ball dip after it crosses the net, allowing you a margin for safety, yet giving your opponent a half-volley or tough low volley if able to get to the ball. You may, in fact, put topspin on passing shots more heavily than with regular ground strokes.

THE LOB

Good lobbing also makes you more effective against a net rusher. An opponent sent scurrying back for some lobs may back off from the net, making it easier for a shot to the feet, the next best thing to a passing shot.

The best players lob often, although their opponents usually have lethal overheads. Average players, on the other hand, are often shaky on the overhead. Assaulted with a series of sky-high lobs, they may put away the first few but then their overheads crumble, dragging down the rest of their games.

Defensive Lobs

The lob can be either an offensive or a defensive weapon. Use defensive lobs to keep yourself alive when you're out of position. Hit each one high and deep, to give your opponent a difficult ball to smash and to gain time to get back in position.

Since a net rusher usually knows a lob is coming if you are scrambling wide, don't bother to disguise the defensive lob. Open the racket face, swing from low to high, follow through, and let your opponent sweat it out, waiting

The lob should resemble an ordinary ground stroke. The racket face opens just before contact.

for the ball to come down. The most common mistake is failing to follow through, so that the ball pops off your racket at random.

Adding a bit of backspin may help you control a defensive lob, but hitting flat works almost as well. Since you are usually on the run, you'll have enough trouble just hitting high enough, without also trying to spin the ball.

Offensive Lobs

Offensive lobs are just as effective as passing shots in winning points outright. When you throw up a defensive lob, you usually have no other choice. When you select an offensive lob, on the other hand, you are in good position and could just as easily hit a passing shot. Ideally, your opponent leans forward, expecting a drive. The element of surprise is working for you. You lift a low trajectory lob just over your opponent's outstretched racket. If you hit too high, your opponent will have time to run back to retrieve the ball. However, don't cut the height too close! If your lob clears your opponent's racket, you'll almost certainly win the point; if it falls short, it's all over.

Here again, disguise is the key. To be most deceptive, prepare early, turning just as you do on passing shots. Start the racket forward with the face on edge, opening the face just before contact to lift the ball and apply slight underspin. Once again, follow through fully to direct the ball.

The topspin lob is a version of the offensive lob that is more difficult to hit. The racket swings sharply from low to high. On the forehand, in fact, the racket often starts rising from below knee level and finishes up over your head or right shoulder. Most players experimenting with topspin lobs don't hit up hard enough, and the ball falls short. The stroke is unnatural for all but western forehanders and a few others. But if you master it, the payoff is tremendous.

After the ball clears your opponent's head, it shoots toward the back fence on the topspin bounce and is almost impossible to run down. You should hit topspin lobs primarily with the forehand. Only a few top players can hit backhand topspin lobs.

A third variety of lob, not in the ground-stroke family but very similar to the offensive lob, is the lob volley, which is usually used in doubles, when all four players are battling it out at close quarters at the net. If one player gets in very close to the net, an opponent opens the racket just before contact and lofts the ball over that player's head.

The lob volley is seldom practiced. It is a situation shot that may creep into your game after you improvise it a few times in the heat of battle.

THE DROP SHOT

On a drop shot, you "drop" the ball just over the net, hoping that your opponent won't get to it or will just barely reach it. The drop shot works well in a number of situations. It can be used to tire an opponent, to bring a baseline player to the net, to win points outright when an opponent is slow in moving forward or is out of position, or to substitute for the approach shot.

A tailor-made situation for a drop shot occurs when your opponent is far out of court and hits to well inside your service line. If you hit a good drop shot, it's a sure winner. But a *bad* drop shot is equally certain disaster. The opponent who gets to the ball early has been handed the net position. You'd have been far better off hitting a more conservative approach shot. The drop shot requires a good deal of racket control, so the conditions must be just right. The trademark of an immature player is attempting drop shots that work only one in ten times.

Kinds of Drop Shots

There are two types of drop shots, each requiring a distinct stroke. The first is used to drop slow balls descending from the peak of the bounce. Take your normal backswing for forehand or backhand. As on the lob, open the racket face just before contact to impart underspin, accelerating the racket slightly to make the ball clear the net. The most common mistake on the drop shot is telegraphing your intention by opening the racket face too early. The drop shot is, in effect, a mini-lob, but your goal is to keep it as short as possible, rather than deep.

The second kind of drop shot is used on rising balls. These shots require excellent timing and a simple stroke like the swing on waist-high volleys. The racket head is slightly open, the backswing and follow-through abbreviated. Meet the rising ball gently. It automatically leaves your racket with backspin that makes it die when it crosses the net.

The Dangers of Drop Shots

The number of "don'ts" on this list indicates how dangerous the drop shot is.

- Don't make drop shots from behind your own baseline unless your opponent hates to play the net.
- Don't drop overheads or other shots that can be put away easily.
- Don't use a drop shot on critical points unless the situation is perfect.
- If you don't know what to do with a shot, don't drop it. Many players use the drop shot in desperate situations when they really should hit deep to gain the time to get back in position.

Set aside some practice time for the shots described in this chapter. They deserve it. The return of serve may be the most important part of your game. The need for effective approach shots, passing shots, and lobs arises every time you play. And, finally, the drop shot gives you further variety.

Preparation for the drop shot should not vary from the player's normal stroking pattern (A). The racket face opens just before contact and slides under the ball to impart underspin (B). A short follow-through is necessary to maintain control of the stroke (C).

A

B

C

7

Continental and Western Styles

In the first six chapters, we have described the classic tennis techniques chosen by many of America's good players, techniques using eastern grips on the forehand and backhand and continental grips on the volley, serve, and overhead. About half of all tournament players fit the classic mold. The other half do just as well with less orthodox styles.

The eastern grips yield the quickest and best results for the largest number of players. They work just as well on high or low balls, on topspin or underspin shots. Moreover, using the eastern grips usually shapes your game into an "eastern" style, molding the contour of your swing, the way you step before hitting, the type of spin you use, and so on. In this chapter we take up the leading alternatives to the eastern style, the continental and the western styles. If you play for a while with one of these grips, your game takes on a continental or a western look.

Regardless of the style they use, we have seen that all good tennis players have certain things in common. They prepare early, position themselves carefully, stay in balance, and follow through whenever possible. What varies, depending on the grip, is the shape of the backswing, the angle be-

Distinctive playing styles are common among top players. When he played, Bjorn Borg was known for hitting his forehands with an open stance and a semi-western grip.

tween the racket shaft and the forearm, and the path of the follow-through. If the timing is right and the racket face nearly perpendicular to the court, you can hit the ball with any grip. Good players often make small grip adjustments to hit specialized shots. For example, a player who drives the ball with an eastern forehand grip may shift to a western forehand grip to hit a topspin lob.

If you do the fundamentals well and are happy with your style of play, stick with it. An unusual stroke or two may be helpful, disguising the direction of shots your opponent could read from an orthodox swing. If you are progressing too slowly, take a close look at your form. A change in your style, such as a grip adjustment, may put you back on the right path.

THE CONTINENTAL STYLE

The continental style is too common among top players to be called unorthodox. For years it has been the choice of Europe's tennis coaches and stars. Many good players of all nationalities start as "easterners" but change grips for the different strokes less and less the longer they play, gravitating, in effect, to the continental style.

Types of Grips

There are three types of continental grips: (1) The full continental, which resembles the eastern backhand grip; (2) the weak continental, which borders on the eastern forehand grip; and (3) the regular continental, which falls between the eastern forehand and backhand grips.

The full continental grip is effective for serve, volley, overhead, and backhand. The forehand is the problem, because the racket face opens, lofting the ball long unless you compensate with a risky flick of the wrist. The weak continental grip is poor for the backhand and backhand volley, fair for the serve and overhead, and good for the forehand and forehand volley. On the backhand, you should put more support behind the racket handle by turning the grip toward the eastern backhand. The regular continental grip gives you the best all-around performance. From now on, we will talk only about the full and the regular, treating them, for simplicity, as if they were one grip, the continental.

The major advantage to the continental grip is that you can use it on all your shots. Once you've got it, you keep it. Continental players avoid a pitfall of eastern stylists, who often mis-hit when caught with the wrong grip in returning hard-hit balls.

The continental's biggest disadvantage is that, on both forehand and backhand, your racket face is open as you bring it forward to meet the ball. You must rotate your wrist to straighten your racket face to hit flat or topspin drives. If you are strong enough, you may be able to keep the racket face perpendicular to the court throughout the swing, but the strain may stiffen your stroke. The mark of a good continental player is the ability to hit loose but controlled ground strokes with good wrist action. The wrist, then, plays a much larger part in the continental swing than it does in the eastern stroke.

A continental player who can't learn to make these delicate wrist adjustments will slice both forehand and backhand, hitting long when playing all hard attacking shots. The forehand is especially erratic if it doesn't consistently carry topspin. An open racket face helps you scoop up low balls but hinders you in attacking shoulder-high shots. You can overcome these obstacles, but it takes practice.

On the continental forehand, moreover, the racket head is much farther above your hand than on the eastern forehand, making it more difficult to get the racket under the ball to hit topspin. Bending the knees, however, helps you drop the racket low enough.

The Forehand Stroke

The continental player's ready position is identical to the eastern player's, except that the racket should point to the net post to your left. Holding the racket at dead center puts unnecessary strain on the wrist.

On the backswing, the racket follows the same path on the continental as it does on the eastern forehand. A semicircular backswing gives you the momentum needed to hit the ball firmly. Since your wrist is on top of the handle rather than behind it (as on the eastern forehand), you will feel some wrist strain at contact, so be sure to take a full backswing to generate enough racket-head speed to hit a forcing drive. Continental players with short backswings often chip the ball. Take full advantage of the free-swinging action the stroke allows. Make every effort to develop the topspin drive, dropping the racket head below the level of the ball before swinging forward.

The moment of truth arrives at the point of contact. Your wrist should be firm, your racket face perpendicular to the court. You meet the ball directly in front of your midriff, slightly later than on the eastern forehand, where you contact it off the left foot. If you meet the ball too early, the racket face will veer to the left and out of the path of your shot, unless you lay your wrist back uncomfortably. The later point of contact helps your down-the-line shots but hinders your cross-court drives.

Take a long follow-through. The extra-sharp angle between racket and arm points the racket directly up in the air at the end of the follow-through, rather than toward the front fence. The arm may also be a bit straighter than on the eastern follow-through.

The Backhand Stroke

If your grip is a full continental, resembling an eastern backhand, you have good leverage for a backhand stroke. But if the U of your hand is on top of the racket in the regular continental position, you can get more support by turning your hand a bit to the left toward the eastern backhand; or you can slice the ball.

Many top continental players do just that, and their slices are often so deep and consistent that they are difficult to attack. Because it opens the face naturally, the continental grip is ideal for slice backhands, whereas the eastern backhander, whose wrist is more locked, has trouble opening the face to slice.

To hit topspin backhands with a regular continental grip, rotate the wrist forward during the backswing or roll it at impact. The former requires great strength, the latter exact timing. In the long run, you are better off using the

slice as your regular backhand and sneaking in an occasional topspin shot to keep your opponent off balance. A relatively flat slice can be used to attack.

THE WESTERN STYLE

A "western style" player is simply one who uses a western forehand grip, with the palm of the hand practically underneath the racket. The western forehand grip is useless on the serve and awkward on the volley. On the backhand, most "westerners" either change to the eastern or continental grip or hit with two hands.

The western forehand can be absolutely devastating. The grip naturally closes the racket face, allowing you to hit with tremendous topspin. It is particularly effective in driving shoulder-high balls. The heavy topspin causes many shots to land short, but after the bounce, the topspin carries the ball high over the baseline, giving the effect of depth.

The major problem the western stylist faces is making the large grip changes needed to play the other strokes. For the eastern player, these adjustments are small enough to be learned with ease. The westerner, on the other

While the continental player (far left, John McEnroe) does not look radically different from the eastern, the western players (center, Andre Agassi, and left, Michael Chang) are easily spotted by their distinctive form.

hand, must reprogram on each shot. As a westerner, if the rest of your strokes are far weaker than your forehand and the gap is widening, change the grip toward the eastern forehand. Otherwise you may remain a one-sided player, vulnerable to attack on the weaker side.

The Forehand Stroke

The backswing for the western forehand may be either straight back or semicircular. The straight backswing is the quickest way to bring the racket head under the ball. Since the racket face is closed, the swing must go from low to high to lift waist-high shots over the net; on higher shots, the closed face simply directs the ball down into the court. But the semicircular backswing is better because it produces more power. The elbow usually leads on the backswing, forcing the racket to whip forward and over the ball, generating heavy topspin that keeps the ball from sailing out. Against hard shots, however, especially fast serves, you may hit late or off center.

As a western player, your footwork may differ from that of the eastern or continental stylist. Many westerners hit with an extremely open stance, playing even shots directed right to them off the right foot instead of stepping with the left like eastern and continental players. The open stance permits you to rotate your shoulders fully as you hit. This body torque generates power and, if under control, can be a big asset.

You should meet the ball far in front of the body, with your racket rising to impart topspin. If you hit late, the shot will be too flat. Balls that bounce waist high and higher are treats for the western player. If you let the ball drop below knee level, you will have trouble scooping it up.

On the western follow-through, the racket takes one of two paths, depending on the height of the ball. On low shots, pull up sharply to make sure your shot clears the net. The racket may even finish over your right shoulder. On high balls, hit straight through the shot. The racket face naturally closes a bit on the follow-through.

The Western Grip

True western players once used the same grip on both forehand and backhand. On the backhand, they twisted the arm to hit with the same side of the racket they used on the forehand. This backhand, of course, is obsolete, having been largely replaced by the two-handed backhand, the best complement to the western forehand. Owing to the recent popularity of the two-handed shot, the western grip is being used more and more frequently. Put the two strokes together, and you can develop an awesome ground game.

However, the western grip has one big disadvantage: It is very awkward on the volley. Opening the racket face to hit underspin, especially on low balls, is a real chore. On higher balls, the racket face closes and punches the ball too short. On the backhand, the two-handed volley limits your reach and cramps your swing on balls that come right at you. And on the serve and overhead, the western grip restricts the wrist snap and produces very flat shots.

Make every effort to learn the continental grip for serving and net play, keeping the western and two-handed grips on the ground strokes.

UNORTHODOX PLAYERS

Ninety-nine percent of your opponents will fall into the categories discussed so far. From time to time, however, you will meet a truly unorthodox player, one who can totally baffle you the first time you face each other across the net. So you'll have some idea of how to retaliate, let's look at two of the most unusual styles.

A number of players who take up tennis at a very early age use two hands on both forehand and backhand. Since their reach is restricted on both sides, you should hit wide to make them run and stretch. (The biggest two-handed stars, incidentally, have usually been specialists in doubles, where they have less court to cover and can get the most out of their strengths—very accurate or forcing service returns and well-disguised ground strokes and volleys.)

Perhaps the rarest style of all is that of the ambidextrous player who has two forehands and no backhand. Occasionally, this style has carried players to the U.S. Championships. How to play a no-backhander? When your opponent is on the baseline, figure out which forehand is weaker and attack it; when your opponent is at the net, often hit the ball right to the body instead of risking a passing shot, since the ambidextrous player often has trouble switching hands in time to volley well.

If you have an unorthodox shot that works and feels comfortable, stick with it. If you change it to a more standard but less natural stroke, it could actually get worse. The game is full of western forehands, continental backhands, and eastern volleys that work beautifully because they feel right. On the other hand, if your unorthodox shot is letting you down, don't hesitate to change to something more classic.

Competition

Your competitive tennis career may consist of an annual showdown with your brother or sister, a weekly battle with your Spanish professor, a summer round of local tournaments climaxing with a shot at the city championships, or a year-round livelihood that takes you to tournaments throughout the world. As a beginner, you'll have your hands full just returning the ball and may not even want to bother keeping score. But as you progress, you'll want to see how you stack up against other players.

Most players, from the Wimbledon champ to the hacker, would rather win than lose. When two rivals square off for a match, they rely on skills that include natural ability, good strokes, desire to win, courage, fitness, speed, strength, experience, and concentration. The trick to winning is to keep adding new weapons from this list to your arsenal and to keep sharpening the old ones.

Two players often bring very different sets of skills to a match, rendering it a toss-up. Take, for example, a contest between a good sixteen-year-old high school player and a crafty fifty-year-old veteran. The younger player is stronger, fitter, faster, and has better technique. The veteran, because of past experience, is able to concentrate

In the heat of play, control and concentration are everything.

longer and has the courage to hit harder when the match gets close. Perhaps one player's burning desire to win will provide the edge.

To get the most out of your game, you must have confidence in it. Confidence is not the same thing as cockiness. It is the product of all the hours you spend perfecting your strokes and positioning. It is the feeling you get when your shots start dropping into the court consistently, even when you hit hard. Your fears begin to disappear. You become certain that your strokes won't desert you when the score gets close.

YOUR FIRST TOURNAMENT

Many serious players enter their first real tournament—whether a club championship or one sanctioned by your regional Tennis Association and open to a large number of players—within a year or two of taking up the game.

Say you've just arrived at the site of your first tournament. The first thing you notice is that most of the people seem to know each other. This reunion produces an endless stream of chatter. The big topics are usually the tournament draw, the inequity of the seedings, recent injuries, and how tough the players are getting. In the olden days, it was easy to tell if you had a difficult match. If your foe wore a shirt embossed with a crocodile or another equally prestigious emblem and carried two rackets, you had to watch out. Today, hackers whose only coordination is in the colors of their shorts and shirts show up regularly at tournaments with a brace of graphite rackets. (It is a bad omen, however, if your opponent happens to endorse his or her own line of equipment.)

Tournament tennis generally brings out either your best or your worst. Many players who look like world-beaters fall apart when the first ball is served. Others who appear harmless reach their peak in the clutch. The best competitors don't sulk, cope well with conditions, and learn from their losses.

DEALING WITH TOURNAMENT CONDITIONS

Adjusting to different court surfaces and types of weather is part of the fun and challenge of competing. Although the dimensions of all courts are the same, switching surfaces may alter your tennis game as much as shifting courses changes your approach to golf.

At the U.S. Open Championships the surface changed within five years from grass, to clay, to hard courts—but one man, Jimmy Connors, won on all three. Although this adaptability is rare, it is a good goal to aim for.

Court Surfaces

The surface you're playing on—cement, clay, grass, or carpet—influences the way you approach a match as much as the style of your opponent does. The surface may determine whether you attack or defend, serve with heavy or light spin, take a short or a full backswing, skid or stop abruptly. Before analyzing their effects on your game, let's look at the categories of surfaces you'll encounter.

Although there are dozens of court surfaces under many brand names, they all may be classified as either hard or soft. Hard courts are made of such materials as cement, asphalt, carpet, wood, and dozens of synthetic materials, usually hard-rubber compounds. Soft courts are made of clay, or a green claylike fast-drying substance, or grass. Different types of hard or soft courts may be slow, fast, or medium, depending on how the ball bounces: On a fast court, the ball skids; on a slow court, it bounces up gradually; on a medium one, it bounces at a speed somewhere in between. There are many combinations of hardness and speed. Wood, for example, is a fast hard court, grass a fast soft court; synthetic is a slow hard court, clay a soft slow one.

Hard courts, which are expensive to build but cheap to maintain, are the most widely used surface in the United States, the choice of clubs, schools, and parks. Sure footing and consistent bounces are among the advantages to hard courts. (Synthetic courts, moreover, give a little underfoot, cushioning you from the jolts you would get dashing about other hard courts.) Perhaps the fastest hard court is polished cement. The ball skids so much that you have little time to prepare, allowing a player equipped with a hard serve and volley and mediocre ground strokes to annihilate an all-around opponent. Attack whenever possible on a fast hard court. Shorten the backswing to meet the ball well in front.

Most hard courts are medium speed because they have some grit to the surface, rewarding players who blend offensive and defensive skills. This variety makes things interesting for players and spectators alike. Whereas on polished cement even routine shots go for winners, on most hard courts a crisp shot is needed to end the point. To play well on hard courts, work on every phase of your game.

Soft courts are traditionally clay or grass. There is only one slow soft court: clay. Clay courts put a much higher premium on defensive play and counter-

punching than do hard courts. A hard erratic hitter may kill a steady defensive player on a hard court but be killed by the same player on clay.

The serve, unless it is a powerhouse, loses most of its steam on clay. It digs in on the soft court and slows down, allowing the receiver to return with a full, unhurried swing. All your other shots slow down as well. A quick opponent runs down even your best shots.

Keep unforced errors to a minimum on clay. You can't atone for a miss by blasting a serve to get the next point cheaply. To win, you must be patient and persistent, often hitting fifteen or more balls on one point. Unless you eventually attack on clay, the points may go on forever. But come to the net sparingly, on short easy balls you can convert into strong approach shots, for with the slow bounce, anything less makes you a sitting duck for a passing shot.

Playing grass courts means playing many low-bouncing and unpredictable balls (far left). On clay courts you must slide into the ball (center). On hard-surface courts (left) the footing is best, the bounces highest.

The footing on clay takes some time to master. On hard courts, you stop and start quickly and change direction easily. On clay courts, you slide as you near the ball. Also, the amount of slide increases from hour to hour as the clay dries out. Experience will tell you when to put on the brakes. Don't lean left or right before the ball is hit, because sliding delays reversing your direction, particularly at the net, where quickness is essential.

Clay courts are well suited to players using a variety of spins. Kick serves jump higher and drop shots die more quickly. In the style of the great clay-court players, use spin both to control the ball and to upset your opponent's rhythm.

Grass is the only fast soft court. Although grass courts are so expensive to keep up that very few players use them regularly, they put up as tough a test as any court surface. If you hit the ball hard, it skids very fast. If you hit the ball gently, it barely bounces. An underspin approach shot stays within a few inches of the ground. On grass the bounce is much lower than on any other surface. The skidding bounce, moreover, rewards aggressive serve-and-volley play sprinkled with drop shots and drop volleys. Another reason to get to the net is purely negative: to hit the ball before it has a chance to take a bad bounce, one of the hazards of grass. When you run, of course, you must slide.

Balls

The balls you use for a match may have almost as much effect on the play as the court surface. Fairly light, pressurized balls are the norm in this country. They favor the offensive player. In most foreign countries and a few parts of the United States, players use heavier balls that are sometimes pressureless. They slow down your shots, forcing you to swing harder or wait more patiently for a chance to attack.

High altitude will affect the player; it also affects the flight of the ball. The thinner air offers less resistance, so the ball flies from your racket and comes back at you very quickly. It generally takes a day or two to get used to the faster game. Most very high areas now use balls that are specially pressurized, so the adjustment is less dramatic.

The amount of humidity also changes the speed of the ball. On muggy days, the ball travels far more slowly than on crisp, dry days.

The Elements

The weather can be so harmful to your game that you may play your best tennis where it doesn't affect you: indoors. With no sun to blind you and no wind to distort the flight of the ball, your timing has to be better. The clear sound produced when your opponent hits helps you anticipate the shot. Add controlled temperature and good lighting, and conditions are near perfect. The other side of the coin, of course, is that you have to make adjustments for sun, wind, and temperature when you play outside.

First, consider sun. If you play during the hour or so each day when your regular service toss is right in line with the sun, change your position along the baseline, adjust your feet, redirect your toss, or use any combination of the three to get a clear view of the ball. For example, you can stand farther to the right than usual, move your right foot farther behind you, and toss to the right of the sun. With practice, these changes will barely affect your serve. Nevertheless, on some very bright days you will be momentarily blinded, so stay in the backcourt for a moment to let your eyes adjust. It's hard to volley when you don't see perfectly.

Playing in the wind is an art and a test of your adaptability. Like favored thoroughbreds defeated by a slow track, many top players have been upset in heavy winds. Be prepared to change your style a great deal. If you generally use a high service toss, lower it to keep the ball from blowing around. When you are playing with the wind, use topspin on serve and ground strokes to keep the ball from sailing out. When playing against the wind, hit higher, harder, and flatter on all strokes, since the wind brakes the ball. Slice serves seem to cut through the wind better than topspin serves.

A crosswind is usually the trickiest type of all. Put it to your advantage by hitting against the wind when playing it safe and hitting with the wind when moving your opponent.

It is possible to play tennis outdoors in extremely cold weather. People may think you're crazy to be out there in the winter, but in dry climates you'll have plenty of company, even when temperatures dip into the 30's or 20's. Wear several layers of sweaters and sweatshirts, and peel them off as you play. Your hands will be cold at first, but they'll warm up after ten or fifteen minutes.

Unusually hot days take their toll of every player. Still, you will hold up well if you get in the best shape possible and, on the court, conserve energy by walking slowly between points and during changeovers. Throughout the match, slowly sip water or a high-energy drink. Hang in there; no matter how badly you feel, your opponent may feel worse.

If you compete often, bad weather will occasionally force you to leave the court during a match. When you start again, you usually get only a few minutes to warm up, so stay comfortable and loose during the delay by wearing a jacket and doing a few exercises.

MAINTAINING FITNESS

A fit tennis player combines speed, endurance, flexibility, and strength with a minimum of weight. The best place to get in shape is right on the court. An hour of drills or playing conditions you for tennis just as well as running several miles does.

Exercise

Most serious players exercise independently as well, particularly during the off season. A sensible conditioning program might begin about three months before a tournament. For the first several weeks, on alternate days, run for distance and, if you wish, work out with light weights to build flexibility and strength. Increase the distance and speed of your runs as time goes on. Buy a good pair of running shoes and try to jog in picturesque areas to relieve boredom. If you choose to lift weights, a regimen many top players swear by, be sure to get a program designed by an expert.

After a few weeks, start sprinting every other day to improve your speed. Sprinting 100 yards, then jogging 100 yards, is grueling but beneficial. Ten of these sets will make you stiff for a few days, but within a couple of weeks the stiffness disappears. Shuttle races and running sideways and backward also improve your ability to move. On alternate days, build up strength by continuing weight training or doing such exercises as sit-ups, leg lifts, push-ups, or others for the abdomen and back, where strength is needed to serve hard throughout a long match.

At the start of a tournament season, if you have a lot of energy and natural speed, you may abandon your training routine altogether. If you are tiring during matches, however, take up a light physical fitness program again. In either case, if you enjoy running, keep it up on days when the weather keeps you off the courts.

Preparing for a Match

On match days, develop a routine that makes you feel alert, comfortable, and ready when you start competing.

Wake up at least three hours before a morning match and eat a good breakfast. If you play in the afternoon, eat a big breakfast and a light lunch. If you don't eat, you may run out of steam in a long match.

Warm up before walking out on the court with your opponent. (The five to ten minutes of official warm-up allowed in most tournaments is usually not enough.) It may take you as little as ten minutes to warm up or as much as an hour, but for most people, about thirty minutes does the trick. If it is not possible to rally with someone, at least hit some balls against a wall or do some light running and exercises to get the kinks out. You simply cannot afford to dump the first set because you're too cold to find your feel for the ball. Tie breakers (see appendix) have made matches much shorter, so you must get down to business quickly.

If possible, watch your opponent play before your match. It is reassuring to walk on the court with a plan in mind. Look for weak points in your opponent's game. Is the forehand shaky? Does the serve always go to the same spot? Is the overhead erratic? Any of these clues will help you.

If you haven't seen your opponent play by match time, watch especially carefully during the warm-up. Another hint on the warm-up: Hit each shot, including plenty of overheads and serves.

Finally, know your options on the spin of the racket that occurs before you play. If your opponent wins the spin and chooses to serve, you choose the side; if your opponent chooses the side, you have the option to serve or receive. If you win the spin, you have the same options. Or you can make the other player choose.

Good singles players know that if they keep fighting even when they are behind, they might just win.

Singles

You are alone on your side of the singles court. There is no partner to come through for you in tight situations, nothing to rely on but your own strokes, fitness, tactics, and mental toughness. You can, however, enlist an invisible ally: the tennis scoring system. Because of its unusual design, it helps you if you follow two rules: Keep fighting, because you always have time to come back, and play the big points carefully.

PLAYING THE SCORE

In tennis scoring, there are no knockouts or time clocks to stop the action. You just keep playing until one player wins two sets (or three, in some major tournaments) by being the first to reach 6 games in each (see appendix). The tie breaker used if the score gets to 6–all is the only factor that limits the length of a match. In many sports, a team or player staging a comeback can run out of time. In tennis, the game simply goes on and on. Every tennis player has had the thrill of pulling a win from a seemingly hopeless defeat. In every tournament there's at least one awkward-looking player who hangs in there, wins a few big points, and eventually disheartens and beats the smooth-stroking opponent.

The importance of the points in a match varies a great deal. Match point in a close third set is crucial; at 5 games to 0, a 40–0 point is of minor importance. These extremes obviously call for different approaches—caution on match point, more daring at 5–0, 40–0. Within a game, there are major and minor points as well. If you play according to the score, you'll know when to bear down and when to relax a little.

Thirty–fifteen may be the most important point in a game. (To simplify things, let's put your score first.) Playing the 30–15 points well may save you from playing the high-pressure deuce and advantage points. At 40–15, you have a big edge. At 30–30, it's a toss-up. The 15–30 point is also important; you need it to stay alive in the game. Although thousands of games are won from 15–40, put your money on the player who has 40 on the scoreboard.

Reaching 30–15 (or better yet, 30–0) is infinitely easier if you win the first point of a game. From 15–0, you need win only one of the next two points to reach 30–15. From 0–15, if you don't win both of the next two points, you are in danger of losing the game.

Winning game points is your ultimate goal in a game. By concentrating extra hard on the 0–0 and 30–15 points, you usually reach game point before your opponent, so you are not the one who faces the uphill battle.

The game score in a set is also significant. (Remember, your score comes first in the examples.) The games become increasingly important from the seventh game on. At 0–5, there may not even be a seventh game. At 1–5, you lose the set by dropping the game. At 2–4, winning the game keeps you close. At 3–3, it allows you to try for a 5–3 lead instead of playing catch-up.

No matter where you fit in the tennis pyramid, playing your best on the big points can make you a winner. Pick out these points and concentrate on them.

PAPER PERCENTAGES AND PERSONAL PERCENTAGES

The tactics of singles play are easy to figure out. Factors such as the angles open to you or your opponent on a given shot, or the height of the net, dictate where you should hit the ball and position yourself. These tactics are called "paper percentages." However, two factors may force you to deviate from paper percentages and play shots that do not seem logical. They are your opponent's weaknesses and your own strengths, the "personal percentages."

If your opponent has a glaring weakness, play it as often as possible, particularly on the big points. Your own strengths also allow you to follow personal percentages. If you do something particularly well, keep doing it as long as you keep winning points. A blistering second serve may be your regular opponent's most reliable shot, but if you tried it, you'd double-fault constantly. And if the big server let up on crucial second serves, it would mean more double faults, not less. All great players defy the paper percentages at times, producing some of their strongest and most unpredictable shots; too many lesser players lose because they try foolish shots. First, learn to execute the basic tactical patterns; vary them only when you've developed strengths that give you your own set of odds.

THE SERVE

The serve and the return of serve are the two most important strokes in tennis. You need to hit one or the other in the court to get a foothold in every point, something that can be said for no other shot. The best serves are "penetrating"; good serves are "steady." A steady serve is usually a slow one made effective by good placement, consistency, and variety. A penetrating serve has these qualities but is hard to hit as well, making it a deadly weapon.

A penetrating serve usually draws a defensive return. Many players penetrate with the first ball and are content to be steady with the second. But if you develop a second serve that can blast your opponent off the court, you will be tough to beat.

Placement

Whether your serve is penetrating or steady helps dictate where you aim it. A big server's entire strategy may be centered around his delivery.

First, let's talk about placing your serves into the right-hand, or deuce, court. If you have a hard delivery, move the ball around. Slicing wide to the forehand is particularly effective, since it draws your opponent so far out that the court is open for your next shot, no matter where the return of serve goes. This wide serve, however, backfires if hit softly, giving your opponent both an easy forehand and a good angle to hit from. If you are a steady server, then, hit only occasional serves wide to the forehand on the deuce side.

Whether slow or fast, a serve down the center of the court on the deuce side is effective because your opponent is unable to hit the sharply angled returns possible from the side of the court. You are also serving to the back-

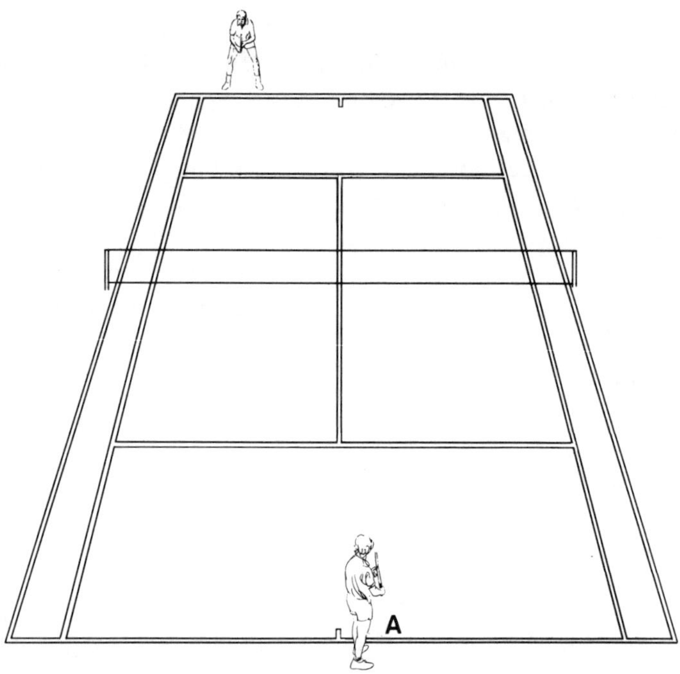

Singles Serving Position. When serving to the deuce court (A), stand close to the center mark. When serving to the backh d court (B), you may stand several feet to the left of the center mark. These positions will give you the best angles to your opponent's backhand.

hand, usually the less dangerous of the two sides, even when it is more consistent. The serve into the body also works well, especially against right-handers, and is probably the most conservative choice; it cramps the receiver, who has to block the ball back, often hitting short. The only problem with a body shot is that it seldom produces service winners.

If you have a penetrating serve, follow the example of top players and hit about 45 percent of your first serves wide to the forehand, 45 percent down the center to the backhand, and 10 percent to the body. If you're a steady server, hit fewer balls wide and more at the body. Regardless of the strength of your serve, hit second serves to your opponent's backhand, unless it is devastating. Once in a while, however, serve a second ball to the forehand to keep your opponent from running around the backhand.

Now let's consider placing your serves in the left-hand, or ad, court. If you have a big serve, hit about 75 percent of both first and second balls to the backhand, 15 percent into the body, and 10 percent down the center. A good

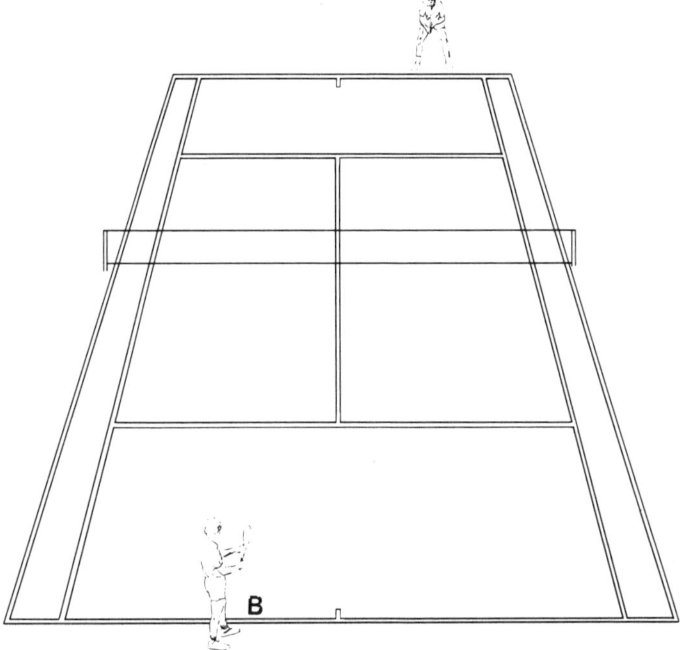

serve wide to the backhand opens up the court. An occasional serve down the center prevents the receiver from standing in the alley and returning your wide serves with forehands. If you have a steady serve, once again, serve fewer balls wide and more at the body.

Where you hit the serve usually dictates the type of spin it carries, since spin and direction are both determined by the angle of the racket. Serves aimed at the backhand are usually flat, topspin, or twist; those hit to the forehand or into the body are mostly slices.

If you are playing a lefty, reverse the ad and deuce courts and follow the same principles of placement, concentrating your attack on their backhands on the deuce side and mixing it up more on the ad side.

As a lefty serving to a righty, you should vary serves to the deuce court and slice to the backhand in the ad court, a serve that works beautifully because it swings so wide. Another strong, often underused weapon is the twist serve to the backhand that breaks into the body.

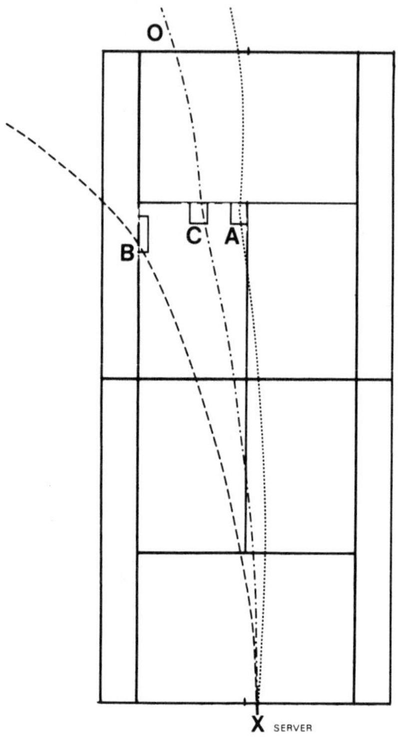

On your first service to the deuce court, a deep serve down the center to the right-hander's backhand is the bread-and-butter stroke (A). A serve wide to the forehand is most effective when hit well short of the service line and close to the sideline to achieve the greatest angle (B). Jamming the receiver (C) often draws a weak return.

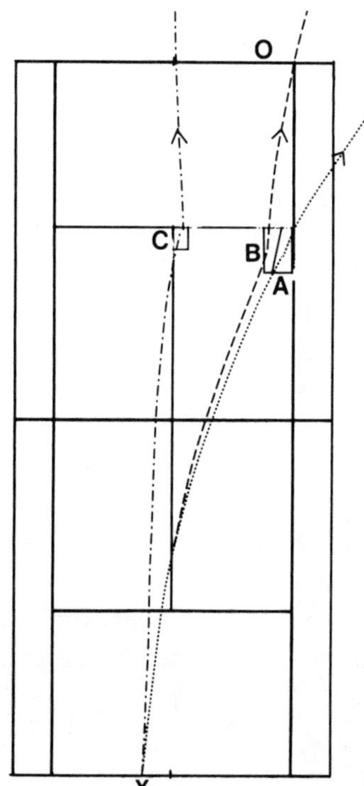

When serving to the ad court, hit the majority of your serves to the backhand. This will often force weak returns and open up the court for the next shot (A). Alternatives are to jam the receiver (B) and to hit the ball deep down the center to the receiver's forehand (C).

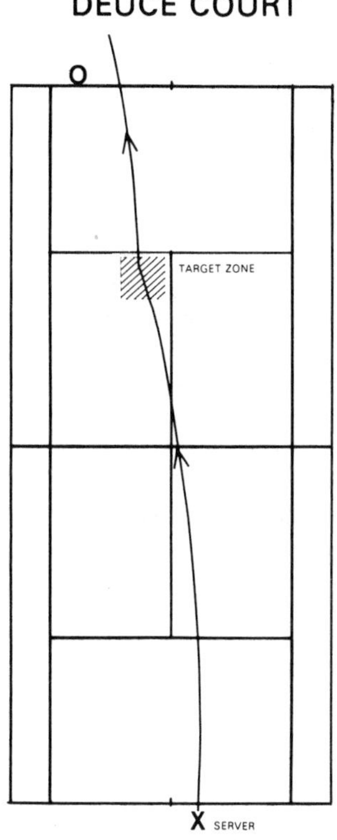

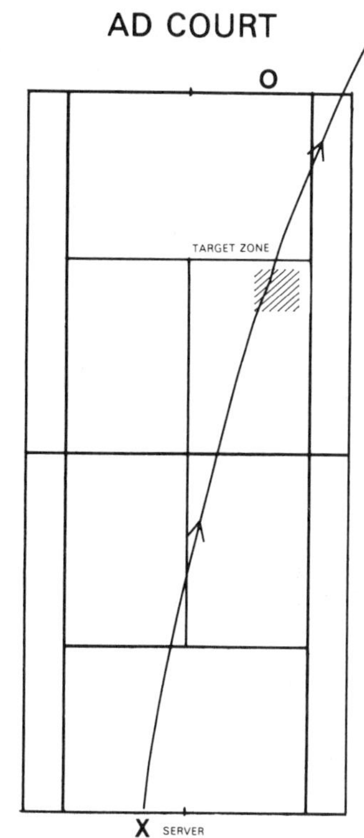

Unless your second serve is fantastic, be content to keep the ball toward your opponent's backhand. Allow yourself more margin for error by using spin and by hitting well within the lines.

As a lefty serving to another lefty, you face the same problem as a righty serving to a lefty: if you don't reverse your regular serving pattern, balls that usually go to the forehand go to the backhand. Some great lefties, unable to serve as effectively as usual, have had trouble against other lefties.

When you are in doubt about where to hit a serve, go for the backhand. Very few one-handed players can hit topspin backhand returns off the normal bounce, which is up around the shoulders, so they slice the ball back instead. While two-handed players do more damage when they have time to set up, they are cramped by serves hit into the body and have less reach on wide serves.

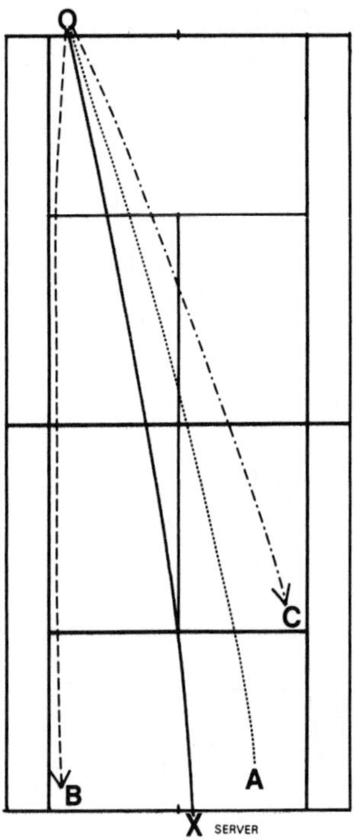

If the server stays at the baseline, the safest return is to play the ball deep down the center over the lowest part of the net (A). The alternative deep return to the backhand is relatively safe (B), but the most difficult shot is a sharply angled cross-court (C), which may open up the court for your opponent's next shot. If the server rushes the net, be sure to keep the ball low.

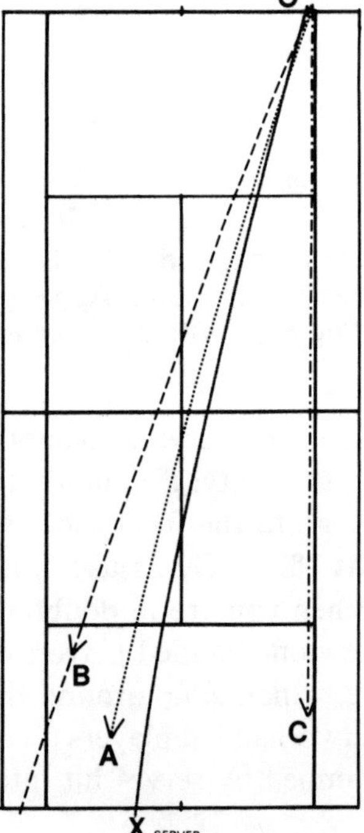

When returning a serve in the ad court, the primary return is down the center (A). The sharply angled cross-court is not nearly as difficult for most players to control in the ad court (B) as the down-the-line (C), which tends to carry wide. If the server is a net-rusher, keep the ball low.

Rushing Net

How often you should rush net behind your serve depends on the strength of your delivery. If you have a penetrating serve that constantly elicits weak returns, you may be able to go in on every serve. If your first or second serve is merely steady, you must use the element of surprise, or your opponent will groove returns that land at your feet. Vary rushing net and staying back so the confused receiver gives you the returns you want: high balls when you come in to volley, short balls when you stay back.

THE RETURN OF SERVE

The type of return of serve you hit depends on three things: (1) Whether your opponent has a steady or a penetrating delivery, (2) whether your opponent serves and volleys or stays back, and (3) whether your return is good enough to go for winners or merely gets the ball back.

Against a big server, just try to get the ball in play at the start of the match. After a while, if your opponent is volleying away the returns, use slice or topspin to keep the ball low, forcing the volleyer to hit up. If you keep popping the ball up instead, or if your opponent has a great low volley, start hitting your returns closer to the lines, especially against second serves. When you hit a good return, take a step or two inside the baseline, positioning yourself to take a short weak volley at the top of the bounce or even in the air.

The safest return is the cross-court shot, since it crosses the net at the center, giving you a low net and plenty of court to hit into. Make the cross-court your bread-and-butter return, using the down-the-line when you're hitting with confidence.

Against a serve-and-volley player with a weaker serve, or a player who stays in the backcourt, hit the return as you would any ground stroke. Keep your opponent on the move, hitting deep and to the weaker stroke, if there is one. If you miss too many returns wide, hit down the middle. Always hit deep. Against weak serves, hit deep with pace; against medium-speed serves, you can use the ball's momentum to return deeper.

BACKCOURT PLAY

There are two kinds of backcourt players. The first is the "pusher," so named because this player clings to the baseline at all costs, rarely takes a chance, and only ventures to the net to shake hands at the end of a match. The other type plays cautious offense, maneuvering opponents from the backcourt until able to force a short ball, which is attacked en route to the net.

Depth

The most important factor in good backcourt play is depth. If you hit the ball deep, you cannot get hurt. Good depth is achieved not by power but by adequate net clearance.

Once you can hit the ball consistently to within 6 feet of the baseline, start placing shots closer to the sidelines and mixing the pace and spin. As a final step, vary the depth to create openings in your opponent's court.

Hitting Cross Court

Cross-court drives—the ground strokes most likely to go in—are the foundation of backcourt play. There are four advantages to playing the ball cross court rather than down the line, even if your opponent is standing on the side of the court you're aiming at:

- The net is 6 inches lower in the center, where a cross-court drive clears it, than on the sides.
- The court is 4½ feet longer from corner to corner than it is down the line.
- If you hit late when aiming cross court, the ball still lands in the center of the court.
- Above all, when you hit a deep cross-court shot, you can recover quickly for the next shot. Simply stay on the same side of the court, moving to a point a few feet from the center mark. If you hit down the line, you must recover to a point well on the other side of the center mark.

There are two exceptions to the cross-court principle. The first arises when one of your opponent's ground strokes is much weaker than the other. If your foe has a strong forehand and a feeble backhand, pound away at the backhand, even if it means hitting down the line. Hit to the forehand only when you can drive the ball into a big opening so your opponent has to hit on the run. Your opponent, in fact, may give you a big hole on the forehand by running around the backhand. (Very few players run around the forehand to hit backhands.) When you hit wide to the forehand, you open up a big hole on the backhand, where you place your next shot to finish off the point. Hitting wide to a strength

—when you can make your opponent run—is one of the best ways to exploit a weakness.

Second, even if your opponent is strong from both sides, down-the-line and cross-court shots work equally well from certain parts of the court, such as behind the center of the baseline, from where the two shots are both quasi-cross courts, and well inside the court, where the net is far less of an obstacle and the difference between the distance cross court and down the line is far less.

Varying Shots

If your opponent thrives on returning crisp drives, alter your tactics to disrupt this rhythm, tossing in a few slices and high-looping shots.

Perhaps the most difficult tactic to execute in the backcourt is varying depth. This means hitting short, sharply angled cross-court shots that pull your opponent far off the court, giving you a large area to shoot for and your opponent a long way to run. These shots can also lure a reluctant volleyer to the net, but if you're not careful you may be feeding your foe a setup—a soft, high shot that he can put away for a sure point.

MID-COURT PLAY

A mid-court shot is one that lands short, on or inside the service line, and that you hit from well inside the baseline. The pusher returns this ball just as gently as any other ground stroke and then retreats to the security of the baseline. The complete player, on the other hand, either attacks this shot on the way to the net or hits an outright winner.

Approach Shots

The primary shot in mid-court play is the down-the-line approach. Stick to the down-the-line shot unless your opponent has a very weak stroke you can exploit by hitting cross court. The advantage to hitting down the line is that you need take only a few steps straight ahead to arrive at the best position at net to cut off the passing shots or, as the diagram shows, to "bisect the angle of the possible returns." Where you stand in relation to where your shot lands reverses when you venture from the baseline to the net. In the backcourt, you hit to one side of the court and await the return on the other. When approaching the net, you hit to one side and stay there. If you direct an approach shot cross court, you must make a mad dash to get into position on the other side of the center line. Your opponent has an enviable choice of passing shots: to hit either down the line, into a big opening, or cross court, catching you running the wrong way.

On a short ball that lands in the center of the court rather than to one side, approaches aimed to either side or straight down the center work equally well. Once again, simply run in, following the line of flight of your shot. If you hit an approach down the center, straddle the center line at the net, leaving your opponent little angle for a passing shot.

Remember, an approach shot simply paves the way for a winning volley. It is not an end-all in itself. Many matches are lost by a player who overhits approach shots. Try to develop a reliable one-two punch with your approach shots and follow-up volleys. It is comforting to know that the point is practically yours every time you get a short ball.

In serve-and-volley play, your first volley or half-volley becomes your approach shot. Don't just serve and charge blindly to within a few feet of the net. You'll miss wide volleys because you can't change direction, and you'll stab

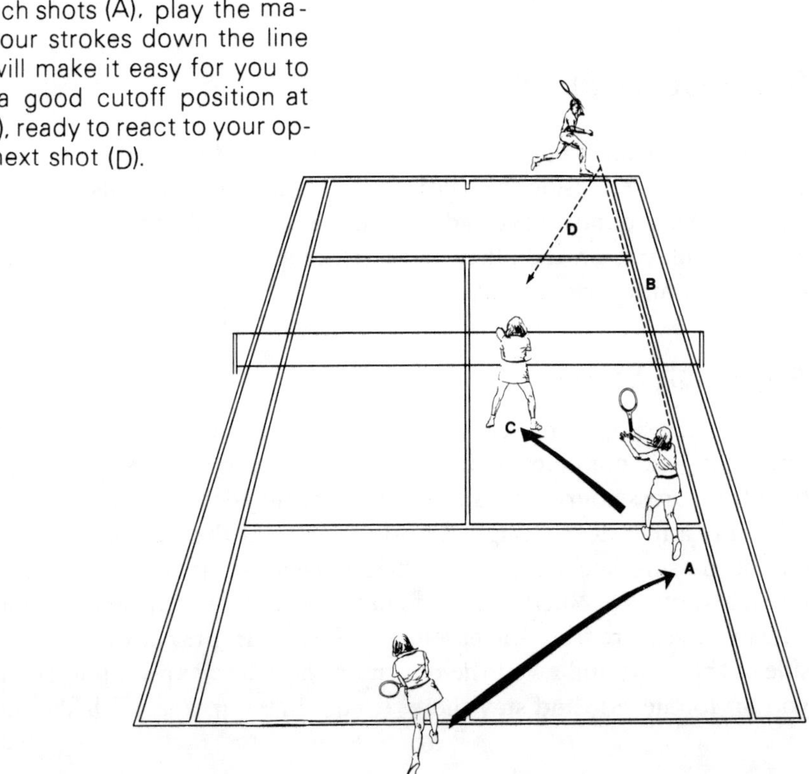

On approach shots (A), play the majority of your strokes down the line (B). This will make it easy for you to move to a good cutoff position at the net (C), ready to react to your opponent's next shot (D).

weakly at volleys within reach because you're moving. Follow the flight of your serve, running at an angle if you serve wide. Watch your opponent as you run, and stop with a hopscotch or a split step just before he or she hits the return. You should get at least as far as the service line, unless you hesitate after the serve or run too slowly. As your opponent's racket starts forward, you're poised to spring right or left to cut off the volleys.

From the service line, hit your first volley either down the line or to the center, just like an approach shot. Then move forward into good volleying position about halfway between the service line and the net. Hit first volleys cross court only when a wide serve opens the court or when your opponent's return of serve is a setup.

The usual ways to reach the net, then, are to approach behind mid-court ground strokes, volleys, and half-volleys. But in special situations there are other ways to come in. Against a weak server, you may rush net after a strong service return. If your opponent hits few short balls, hit a virtual lob from the baseline, a slow, deep, topspin shot that gives you plenty of time to get to the net and forces your foe to generate enough power off a floater to pass you.

Hitting Winners

Although most mid-court shots pave your way to the net, you can also hit them for outright winners, if you have good ground strokes. Save your killer shots for balls that set up short and high. Hit crisply toward the sideline. Deadly execution of these shots is the trademark of many top players, who send opponents running for cover on every short blooper. As on passing shots, the key is disguise, which is achieved by preparing early.

The Drop Shot

Another valuable mid-court shot is a drop shot. A good one wins the point, or at least tires your opponent. Use the drop shot most often against slower opponents who dislike coming to the net. Hit most drop shots down the line, because the ball hangs in the air a shorter time than when played cross court. After you drop-shot, come to the net. Your opponent usually hits up, setting up a volley you can crush.

Put yourself in your opponent's shoes for a moment, and you're faced with another mid-court shot: the return of a drop shot. To win the point, you must hit a near-perfect shot, a chip near the line, or a deft lob. If the drop shotter makes the mistake of staying back, hit slow and deep and go to the net, or play another drop shot, usually a big surprise, since your opponent is probably leaning back waiting for an approach shot.

NET PLAY

You are at the net for one reason—to end the point. You are no longer maneuvering your opponent, as you did from the baseline, or attacking, as you did from mid court.

Although an occasional drop or other sophisticated volley may sometimes be useful, the basic rule of volleying is simple: Hit to the open court!

If you hit the approach or first volley down the line and are fairly close to the net, punch the following volley to the other side of the court. Trying a clever shot to the same side, behind your opponent, usually backfires. If your opponent scrambles over to get the ball back after you hit to the opening, hit the next volley to the new opening, and so on until the point ends. Make this volleying pattern automatic. Just executing a good volley takes all your concentration, so don't confuse yourself with options on where to hit!

On easy balls, whether high volleys or short overheads, angle the shot sharply to either side. On low, difficult volleys in the center of the court, hit to a corner and then volley to the opening you've created. On deeper overheads, hit a medium-paced shot deep and get back to the net. If your opponent hits a series of good lobs and you return them with good overheads, you'll get a setup sooner or later.

If a deep lob goes over your head, your opponent will usually rush net. Run back and send up another high, deep lob. Passing shots are tough to hit off high, soft balls, especially if you're running backward.

Many players reach the top because they know when to play percentage tennis and when to defy the odds. One great, unexpected shot hit at just the right moment might swing a match your way. If you have a winning stroke, use it whenever you can. Singles provides plenty of room for imagination.

Nevertheless, winning in singles is largely a matter of executing the tried-and-true patterns of play better than your opponent, of playing the percentages rather than bucking them.

Keep three basic principles in mind:

- Exploit your opponent's weaknesses.
- When in doubt, hit cross court from the baseline, hit approach shots down the line, and volley to the open court.

- Always change a losing game, never change a winning one.

The last is perhaps the oldest of tennis axioms. Clarence Mabry, the former coach of National Collegiate Champion Trinity University, once used a variation on this saying: "There are a lot of ways to lose, try them all." Do try them all. Your favorite style may be exactly the one your opponent thrives on.

Dominating the net is the key to good doubles play.

Doubles

Once you've learned the basic strokes, it's a joy to play good doubles. Although no match for a professional team in power and reflexes, a club pair may use teamwork that is just as smooth, and their understanding of the game may be just as visible on every point.

GENERAL TECHNIQUES

The techniques of doubles are virtually the same at every level of play, and they are based on one key principle: Dominate the net. Only a handful of winning teams have played primarily from the baseline. The net-rushing approach allows you to finish the points with volleys and overheads. Sticking to the baseline, on the other hand, means that your *opponents* have to *miss* volleys and overheads. In short, take the net to hit winners or force errors.

There are five basic techniques that apply equally to men's, women's, and mixed doubles.

1. Since the serve and the return are the vehicles that take you to the net, they are the "must" shots of doubles. These strokes give you a foothold in a point. If you miss them, your other shots can't

do you any good. Steadiness and placement, rather than speed, make the serve and return effective. Put in a high percentage of first serves to keep from relying on weaker second serves that your opponent may attack en route to capturing the net. A consistent, well-grooved return of serve puts you on even terms with the serving team.

2. Make the opposing team hit the ball up to you. When you and your partner are on the baseline and both of your opponents are at the net, chip or hit with topspin to keep the ball low. The high shots that yield good depth in singles allow the team at net to hit down and put the ball away in doubles. When your team is at the net and one or both of your opponents is back, hit all volleys except setups deep to the baseline player to force high, soft returns. If everyone is at the net, hit to the opposing volleyers' feet, forcing them to pop up a shot you can blast or angle for a winner.

3. Hit down the middle of the court, or between the players when they shift in tandem to one side. The center shot has three advantages: (1) It is the safest one possible—if you misdirect the ball by a few feet to either side, it still goes in; (2) it leaves the receiver little angle on the return volley; and (3) your opponents may be confused over who should take the shot, clashing rackets or letting the ball go by untouched.

4. Move together with your partner. Strive to stay together in the forecourt or backcourt and to move laterally together, keeping a constant distance between you, as if a piece of rope connected one of your partner's ankles to one of yours. Try not to split up so that one of you is at the net and the other back. After you serve or return serve, join your partner at the net. Go back with your partner when he or she retreats to cover a deep lob. When one of you hits wide, follow the shot in tandem to be in the best position to cover the return. When your partner is driven completely off the court, move to the center to provide time to recover.

5. Communication may be your biggest asset. Doubles is a team sport. Talk to your partner; offer praise for good shots, encouragement in bad situations. Keep reminding each other about your game plan, and keep updating it. And obey the principles of percentage play, so that your partner feels supported, not stranded.

SETTING UP A DOUBLES TEAM

Choose someone you get along with as a partner. If your personalities clash, you're likely to end up battling *three* foes.

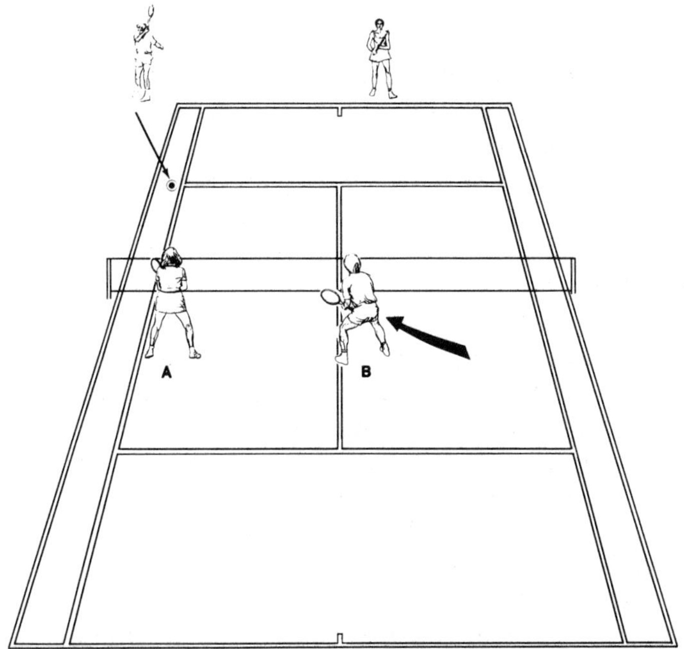

Move with your partner. Since the net player (A) has moved to her left to cover any wide shot, her partner (B) shifts to his left to keep the distance between them equal.

Who Plays Which Court?

Before your first match, you and your partner have some important decisions to make. Perhaps the biggest one is determining who receives in the right and left courts. The most crucial points are the 30–15, 15–30, and advantage points, all of which start off in the left court. If one player is much better than the other, put the stronger player in the left court.

If the partners are about equal, weigh other factors. For example, in a team combining a left- and a right-handed player, usually play the lefty in the left court. In this formation, the forehand volleys, which provide more reach than the backhand, are to the outside. At net, you can stand a step or two closer to a left-handed partner, plugging the hole in the center of the court, and still cut off most wide shots with the forehand. In addition, you will lure your opponents into hitting more low percentage shots to the alleys. Despite the advantages of this formation, however, if one or both of you feel more comfortable with the backhands to the outside, play that way.

If both of you are right-handed and play equally well, analyze your specialties to decide on which side each of you fits best. The left-court player should be quick and powerful, even if erratic. On a lob, the left-court player can cover more court. Since the overhead is to the middle in this court, the left-court player can play all the overheads in the center and just right of center, saving the right-court player from backpeddling awkwardly to take them on the backhand. The right-court player must be consistent, even if a soft hitter and on the slow side. The right-court player sets up the left-court player, who finishes the point.

Another consideration is that a player must be able to return serves cross court, and away from the net person, from the chosen side, especially off the backhand, where most serves are directed. The left-court player seldom has a problem but merely meets the backhand in front, as in hitting cross court in singles. The easiness of this shot accounts for the overabundance of good left-court players. But the left-court player must also master a shot rarely hit in singles, a "reverse cross-court" backhand hit later than a down-the-line shot. This specialty is not as important for intermediates, who get fewer serves pinpointed to the backhand.

Two left-handers should use the same criteria in selecting which court to receive from but should place the player with the stronger overhead in the left-hand court.

Who Serves First?

The better server should be the first to serve, except when the sun or wind will take the sting from the delivery. If you break serve early, you'll have your big gun firing at 5–3 or 5–4. In a set decided by one break, the lead-off server serves three games to the partner's two. Remember that in doubles, but not in singles, you can change the rotation at the end of a set so that the better server always goes first.

The Starting Positions

The standard starting positions at the beginning of a point are as follows:

- Server: Six to 8 feet to the right of the center mark in the deuce court; 8 to 10 feet to the left of the center mark in the ad court.
- Server's partner: Approximately in the center of the service box on the side opposite the server.
- Receiver: Near the intersection of the baseline and the singles sideline.
- Receiver's partner: On or just inside the service line, 4 or 5 feet from the center service line.

DEUCE COURT

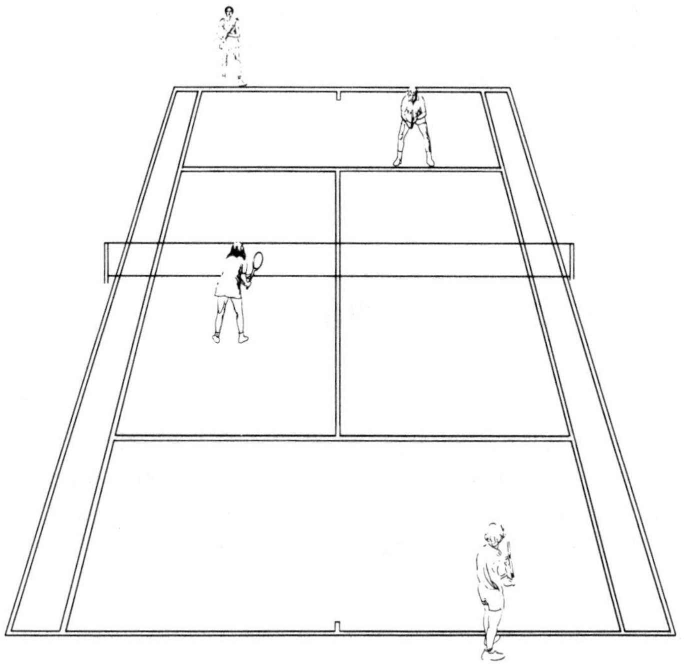

The standard positions each player assumes at the beginning of a point are shown above for the deuce court and below for the ad court.

AD COURT

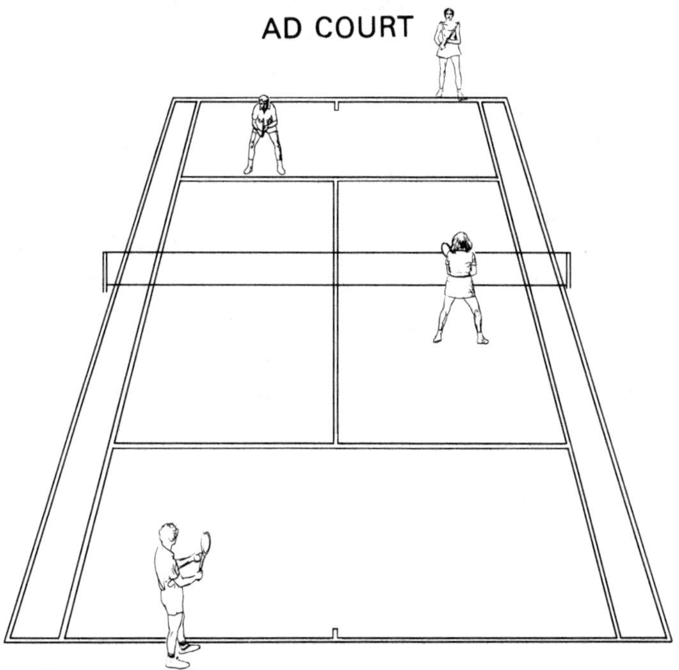

You may vary these positions slightly, adjusting to the strong and weak points of the other players. The server has the least reason to move but may do so to get a better angle to an opponent's weakness. The server's partner may stand much closer to the net if the opposition seldom lobs. The receiver may move if the serve usually goes to the same spot. The receiver's partner may move much closer to the net for a partner with an excellent return of serve.

These are simply variations on the same standard position. Alternative formations are discussed later in the chapter.

THE ROLES OF THE PLAYERS

The Server

The serving team has a big advantage. The pressure is on the receiver, who must return cross court into a small area to keep the net player from intercepting. Meanwhile, the server is running in to volley even a good return, taking the net while the receiver is still in the backcourt. It's easy to see why service breaks are much rarer in doubles than in singles.

Slice or topspin serves are the most effective. You should make about 80 percent of your first serves, and the spin gives you the control to do it. The spin also slows the ball down, giving you time to get close to the net to make a forcing first volley.

In the right court, you should hit mostly down the center or into the receiver's body. Serve wide to the forehand only to keep the receiver off balance or to exploit a very weak forehand. Otherwise, your partner must go out of the play to cover the alley or risk being passed down the line.

In the left court, serve primarily to the backhand, unless it is deadly. Serving to the forehand is safe, however, because the receiver doesn't have much angle hitting from the center of the court.

After the serve, approach the net and play the first volley from well inside the service line, farther in than in singles. Since you have less court to cover, you will also move straight into far more volleys than in singles. If the volley is a setup—a soft, high shot—put it away by hitting by or through the net player. If you get a more difficult shot, such as a wide or low ball, hit a safe volley back to the receiver and close in on the net. Once again, putaways usually are hit to the net player, safe volleys to the receiver. Don't risk blasting the ball, for the receiver is either on the baseline or at mid court and has time to handle almost anything you send across.

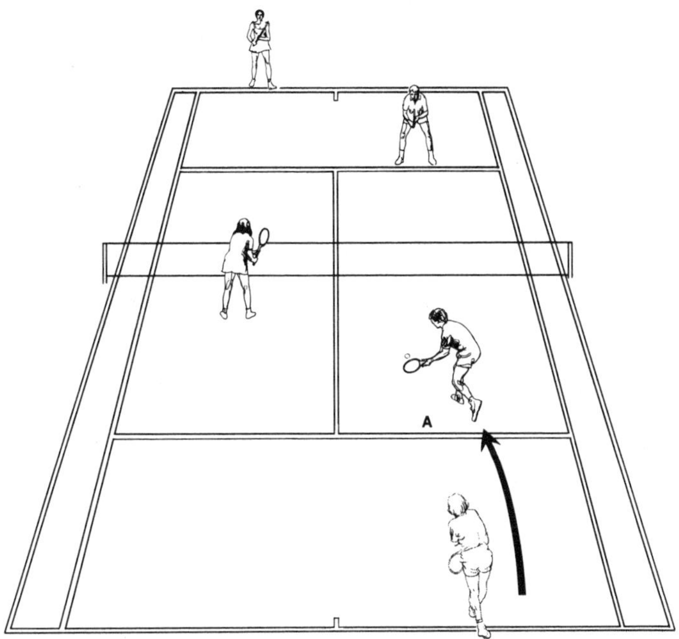

The server's first volley (A) is played from inside the service line whenever possible.

The Receiver

Your primary objective when returning serve is: Don't set up the server's partner! Standing across the net at point-blank range is your own partner, who is counting on you for protection. The standard return in doubles is a topspin drive or underspin chip, aimed low and cross court to make the server volley up. It is usually easier to hit low and short with soft to medium-paced returns.

Your cross-court returns are most effective when mixed with occasional down-the-line returns and lobs over the opponent at net. Hit a few of these shots early in a match to make the server's partner think twice before "poaching," a term for running across the net to intercept a cross-court return. Lobbing, moreover, drives back the opposition and gives you time to take the net.

After returning serve, come to the net, except against a serve so strong that

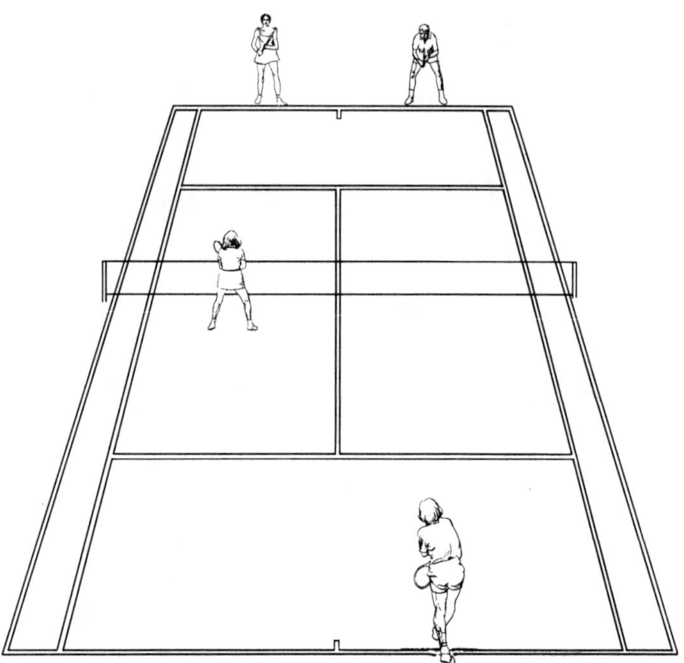

Against a strong serving pair, many teams prefer to stay back to give themselves an opportunity to get into the points.

your returns are too weak to follow in. Even then, get in as soon as possible behind a good ground stroke or lob. There are two problems with staying in the backcourt: It takes the pressure off the server, who can get away with a soft, high first volley, and it leaves your team "split," one player up, the other back, opening a hole behind the net player that makes a perfect target for a cross-court volley from the server's partner. In short, return and get to the net as soon as possible. The team that dominates the net usually wins.

The Server's Partner

As the server's partner, you are first and foremost responsible for covering drives and lobs aimed into your alley. If a drive goes past you into the alley, you've lost the point. If you let your partner take a lob hit over your head after serving, you delay your partner's getting to the net. Simply take any ball hit to your half of the court.

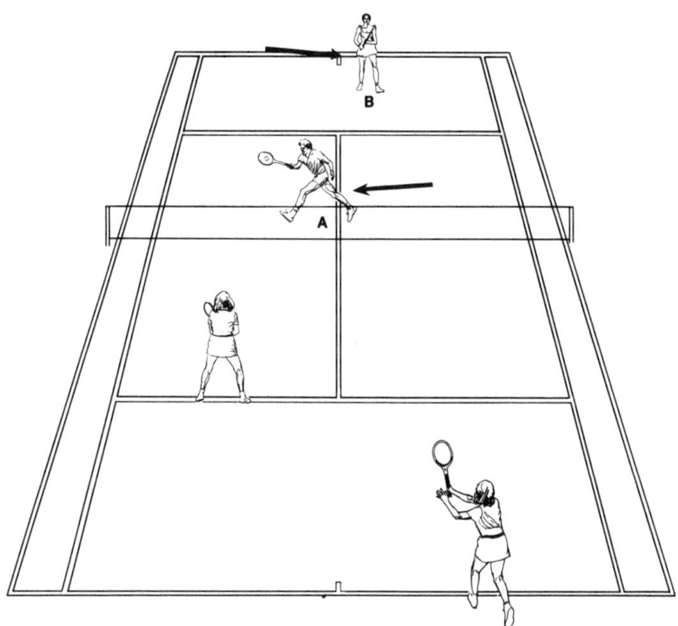

The poaching net man (A) moves across the court to intercept a wide ball. Note that his partner (B) has moved behind him to cover the part of the court he has left open.

Learn to intimidate the receiver with poaches and fakes. There are two types of poaches, a planned and an impromptu poach. On a planned poach, you and your partner agree before the point begins that, just after the serve, you'll run to the other side of the court to pick off the return of serve. Your partner covers for you by moving to the side of the court you've just vacated. The planned poach can be agreed upon by talking between points or by behind-the-back hand signals from the net player. Keep hand signals simple. A closed fist meaning "no poach" and an open one meaning "poach" are sufficient.

On an impromptu poach, you cross over without notifying your partner. Good impromptu poachers read the receivers' intentions by the way they position the body, feet, or racket just before hitting. Poaching is simple when you get a high ball, or blooper, that hangs over the middle long enough for you to run over and kill it. But against good returns, the move to poach must be timed perfectly: If you cross too early, the receiver will notice and hit down the line; if you move too late, you may not get to the ball, and even if you do, your weight won't be behind the volley. You must leave your starting position a fraction of a second later than on a planned poach, waiting until the receiver's eyes drop just before hitting, for an opponent who sees you move will hit down the line into the vacant court.

If your partner has a good serve, you'll be able to dominate the middle by moving over to pick off easy returns. If the serve is weak, you'll spend most of your time cowering in the alley in self-defense.

The Receiver's Partner

As the receiver's partner, stand near the service line in most cases, closing off the diagonal opening between yourself and your partner and giving yourself a play at many of the opposing net person's volleys that would otherwise go directly behind you for winners. If your partner hits a good return, you can—and should—close in on the net with only a few steps. You are even in a good position to poach in case the server hits a weak first volley. At the service line, you are in neutral, poised to go on offense or defense, depending on the strength of your partner's returns.

If almost all these returns are forcing, you may prefer to stand a few feet closer to the net to pick off the server's weak first volleys or intimidate this player into missing more of them.

PLAY AFTER THE SERVE AND RETURN

Once the return is in play, the team that plays better at the net usually wins the point.

Closing

The trademark of a good doubles player is "closing," moving to within a few feet of the net to kill volleys and intimidate the opposition. You should close after you or your partner hits a strong shot likely to force a weak return. The timing of your move is crucial. Close either the instant *after* your opponent hits, when you spot the easy shot, or *before* the racket starts forward, when instinct tells you it's time for a kill. If you move in too quickly, you're vulnerable to a lob. But it's just as bad to hang back in the middle of the service box, letting the ball drop below the level of the net.

Although you and your partner will close together on some obvious kills, only one of you usually does, the one who has just hit and has the momentum.

It's easier to close in doubles than in singles. When your partner is completely committed (by hanging over the net), you can stay put or retreat a step or two to cover a lob.

Learn when to close and when to hold your ground or even retreat a bit, striving to develop a sense of when you are on the offensive and when you are on the defensive.

Split Positions

When both you and your partner are at net and your opponents are split, playing one up, one back, exploit your advantage. Say the opponent opposite you is back. If you get an easy volley, hit through the open diagonal between the two players; if your partner gets the setup, he or she should hit at the opposing net person at point-blank range. If either of you gets a difficult volley, hit deep to the baseline and wait for a better opportunity to put the ball away.

When your team is forced to play one up, one back, hit low shots cross court or down the center; avoid down-the-line balls that expose the open diagonal.

Lobbing and Covering Lobs

The lob is a critical weapon in doubles. You must lob frequently against a good team, even if the players have good overheads. Otherwise they will close in tight on the net and bang down on your attempted passing shots. Another advantage to lobbing is that your opponents will have trouble putting the ball away because the doubles court is far better covered than the singles court. An experienced team often lobs an aggressive young team to death. The smasher's confidence wavers after a while, and once-powerful overheads deteriorate into harmless push shots.

Covering lobs is simple when your team is playing one up, once back. If the ball is lobbed over your head, your partner on the baseline runs over to return it. Switch sides so both of you aren't caught on the same side of the court. Talk to your partner, using such expressions as "switch" and "mine" to indicate what you're doing.

If both of you are at net, cover your own lobs in most cases. On the other hand, if your partner is off balance or can't get back in time, call "Mine!" and cover it yourself.

When covering lobs, both players prepare by moving back immediately. Avoid the one-up, one-back situation.

Call a warning when a lob or any other shot hit to your partner is going out. You can often judge the depth of a ball better when you are not concentrating on hitting it.

ALTERNATIVE FORMATIONS

The most widely used alternative to the one-up one-back starting position is a receiving formation in which the receiver's partner plays back or (a variation) stays back on the first serve and moves to the service line on a weaker second serve. Many top teams use this strategy against a very strong serve.

The disadvantage of this formation is that you are not in position to capitalize on a weak volley from the server. The advantage is that the serving team has trouble putting away even a weak return, and you may be able to work your way into the point with a series of ground strokes and lobs.

A second alternative is the "tandem" formation, in which the serving team's players line up on the same side of the court, the server starting near the center mark, the partner at the net and a few feet to the side.

The tandem formation works best against players who have been riddling you with good cross-court returns. Switching to tandem during a match forces the receiver to return with a possibly weaker down-the-line shot. In any case, this opponent is grooved to hit cross court, and suddenly having to redirect the returns may bring about a miss. You can use a pre-planned poach from the tandem formation to give this receiver one more thing to think about.

Mixing your formations may also disrupt the rhythm of the serving team and give you a long-awaited service break. Experiment with your formations, especially if you're being beaten by the same patterns point after point.

An alternative to the one-up, one-back formation is the tandem pairing, in which both the server and his partner stand on the same half of the court. This is usually done to upset the rhythm of a receiver who is particularly effective in hitting cross court.

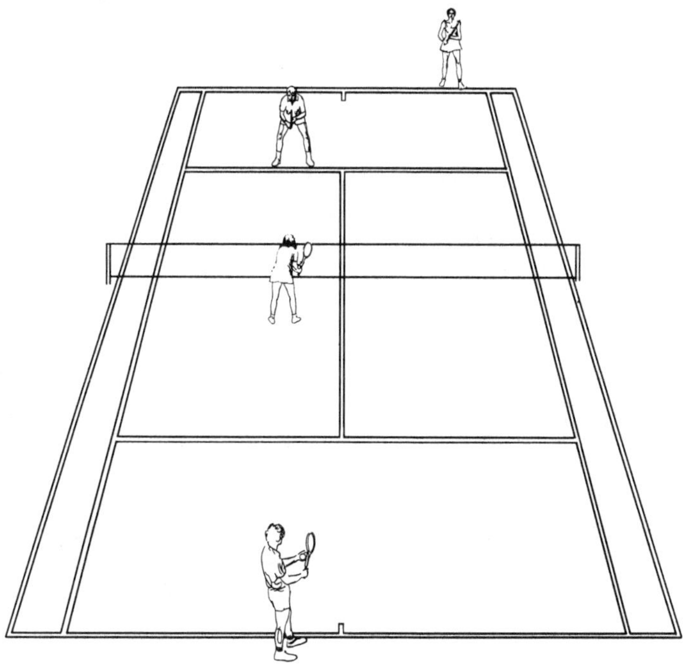

Before stepping out on the court to practice or play, do what the pros do—stretch.

11

Practice

Practice involves much more than the ten-minute warm-up before a match or half an hour of hitting down the center of the court. There is nothing casual about practice. Your sessions should be as well planned as your strategy in a close match. And they should be enjoyable. Each step you take up the tennis ladder, however, requires more intensive effort than the last one. So to make the hard work of practice fun, you must have a strong desire to improve.

Your strengths and weaknesses in practice, usually a result of which strokes you've been working on or neglecting lately, are mirrored in your match play. Everyone has run into the player who misses a crucial but easy forehand volley in a match and appeals to heaven to explain how so easy a shot could be blown. The reason is simple: In the last practice session, this player hit only six out of ten forehand volleys in the court but now expects to make them all under the pressure of competition. It just doesn't work that way. You cannot expect to play much better than you practice.

In your practice sessions, divide your time between two activities: drills, the exercises designed to practice strokes, movement, and tactics, and playing sets and matches. You must decide which you need more. Many people who "just hit" have beautiful strokes but couldn't beat their grandmothers in a match. Your goal is to become a better *player,* not just a better hitter. At the opposite extreme are the players so eager to compete that they refuse to practice enough to correct their weaknesses, severely limiting their potential.

Most players should usually spend about equal time drilling and playing. Stress drilling, however, when you are changing a stroke or trying to find one that is temporarily lost. If you are totally overhauling a stroke or two, you may go further, just doing drills for a few weeks to avoid the temptation of reverting to your old form under the pressure of playing. If you are hitting well but aren't "match tough," play more than you drill.

Play practice sets one way if you are highly competitive yet philosophical about losing, another way if you're less competitive. Those who are stout of heart often work on their weaknesses as they play, even if it means losing. Aiming every second serve deep or driving every return of serve may cost you some practice sets but may make you a better player in the long run. If you compete a bit timidly, go all out to win in practice to fuel the competitive fires.

THE BASIC PRINCIPLES OF PRACTICING

The following basic principles of practicing apply mostly to both drilling and playing sets, with a few obviously applying only to drilling.

Warming Up

Before beginning a strenuous workout, stretch your muscles to avoid injuries. Once on the court, hit softly for the first few minutes, gradually picking up the pace as you get warmed up. You have as much chance of injuring yourself in practice as you do in a match, so loosen up just as carefully. Tough off-court exercises, such as long-distance running, sprints, and weight training, should be saved for after practice. If you do them before, you'll be too tired to give 100 percent on the court.

Placing the Ball

Aim for spots on the court every time you hit the ball. Zero in on the point where the ball must pass over the net to land there. Place convenient targets such as racket covers, towels, balls, or cans on the court. Your percentage of hits and near hits tells you how well you're doing. Give every shot, whether hard or soft, a definite direction and purpose. If you practice enough to groove a cross-court backhand, your racket will automatically move smoothly through that groove when you think "cross-court backhand" in a match. If not, it's back to the courts for more practice. It's a never-ending process. Once you're very accurate, add more power or disguise. You can always learn and improve; the best players seem to work hardest.

Hitting on the First Bounce

Try to hit the ball on the first bounce. Letting the ball bounce twice does you no good because it is legally out of play. In addition, you'll develop lazy footwork, and the spin of the ball changes a great deal after the second bounce. There are two exceptions to this rule. When you rally against the backboard, hitting on the second bounce or later gives you the time you need to prepare, and when you're perfecting a stroke, it saves you from the distraction of chasing around the court. Another lazy practice habit is letting the ball drop far below the top of the bounce before hitting. Hustle to take every ball near the top of the bounce.

Varying Conditions

Practice in all kinds of conditions, particularly if you often play in tournaments. If you have to play a match in a strong wind or on a soggy court, your opponent should be more thrown off by the discomforts than you are.

Practice intensively. A spirited forty-five-minute session does more good than a two-and-a-half-hour marathon that dulls your enthusiasm. If you stay alert and run down every ball, time passes quickly. Have a large supply of balls handy to keep practice moving quickly. Hitting serves by yourself with three balls is more like backpacking than tennis.

Work on every facet of your game. Pay special attention to your weaknesses, but don't forget your strengths. Every shot needs constant tuning to stay sharp. Work on serves and returns, since you can't play without them, and hit plenty of overheads, because the timing is easily lost.

Instruction

If you're receiving instruction, work between sessions on the problem areas your coach or teacher has pointed out to you. Otherwise, your game stands still and you'll get the same tips week after week. Aside from teaching the basic strokes, a tennis pro's most important role is to give you a tailor-made practice routine.

If you are not progressing fast enough despite the instruction, it may be time to change instructors. Give the decision careful thought, because the transition may be confusing. If you do go to a new pro and things don't get better, examine your practice habits to see if *you* are to blame.

PRACTICE REQUIREMENTS

Court

Although you need a full court to play practice sets and to do many essential drills, you can get a good workout on part of a court, or even without one. Don't let foul weather or the prospect of sharing a court keep you from practicing.

If the courts are crowded, try to share one with other players. Half a court is plenty of room to work on every part of your game and is preferable for down-the-line and other drills.

Off-Court Practice

With ball machines, you often don't need a court. To save space, many clubs and tennis camps provide a number of "training alleys," each accommodating one player. Hitting into these narrow corridors requires good control. With a ball machine, a backstop, a few targets, and some ingenuity, you can set up a training alley of your own.

Backboards or hitting walls are among the best learning aids. You can hit at your own pace, and your "partner" never misses. Hit against your garage door, if your neighbors can stand the noise. In winter, practicing in a squash court or against a wall keeps your strokes in shape. An alternative to a hitting wall is a "rebound net" you can purchase. The net requires less area than a backboard because it can be adjusted to absorb some of the ball's pace, reducing the force and distance of the rebound. You can easily fit a rebound net into a porch, driveway, or garage.

Swing the racket in front of a full-length mirror or a picture window. When you step on the court, you'll be surprised at how well you reproduce the strokes grooved in these "shadow drills."

Volleys can be practiced anywhere, if you have a partner. Using good form, keep the ball going back and forth in the air as long as you can in a backyard, playroom, or even a living room (use foam rubber balls to protect the breakables).

If you enjoy running, simulate movements you make on the court by running backward, skipping sideways, and sprinting.

Time

Champions practice every day, staying away from the courts only when they feel that a rest, rather than practice, is what they need to win more matches. Their practice sessions vary in length from less than one hour to almost three hours.

Top tournament players aside, it is nearly impossible to practice too much. Just be sure your practice sessions don't go on and on, causing you to get stale or sloppy.

If you play few tournaments but want to improve, try to practice at least three times a week, even if you simply rally against a wall for twenty minutes or serve a bucket of balls. Try to get in plenty of mini practices by running and doing shadow drills. On days when you have time for nothing else, just pick up the racket and swing it a few tirnes so it won't feel like a club the next time you step on the court.

Partners

Your most valuable hours on the practice court are probably spent with a partner about as good as you are. However, sessions spent with a group, with lesser players, or by yourself all have their place.

If you are in a group of three or more, use a round-robin format so that everyone gets a chance to play or drill against everyone else.

Don't be a snob. You can have a good workout with lesser players. Feed balls to each other, practicing the shots that need work. If you play, be steady. Blasting a weaker player off the court helps nothing but your ego.

Practice by yourself against a wall or with a ball machine. Hit serves regularly. As your serve improves, hit harder and aim closer to the lines. Only regular practice keeps your delivery sharp.

Assemble a list of partners who like disciplined practice. Don't practice solely with players who disdain working on their games and want to play matches every time out. Keep a record of what you do in each workout to be sure you practice each part of your game regularly.

DRILLS

Drills are designed to do three things: groove strokes, improve your movement, and enhance your play in matches. In grooving drills, you repeat the same stroke over and over until the proper form is ingrained. In movement drills, you improve your quickness by running in patterns like the ones a tough opponent puts you through. In match-play exercises, you execute tactics until they become second nature when you play matches. Some routines are hybrids, combining something taken from two of these drills, or all three.

Although you should use all three types of drills at times, spend most of your time on the ones that focus on your weaknesses. For example, if you have beautiful strokes that abandon you in matches, do a lot of match-play drills. If you lack smooth strokes or quickness, concentrate on the others. You may even invent some drills to shore up a weak stroke.

To get you started, here are a few drills from each category.

Stroke-Grooving Drills

1. The hitting wall can be used to practice every stroke. On ground strokes, start a few feet from the wall, hitting very gently to gradually adjust your timing. Then move way back, about 40 feet if there is room, and let the ball bounce twice before hitting. The double bounce, usually taboo, gives you time to use proper footwork and a smooth stroke.

Although volleying against the wall is tiring, it develops strength in the grip and arm. Start close to the wall and hit softly. If you can keep the ball going, move back and hit harder.

If you want to serve and a court is unavailable, serve against the wall, aiming for targets such as boxes drawn in chalk. After putting the ball in play with your serve, finish some imaginary points.

Practice the overhead by bouncing the ball hard with a service motion, so that it hits a few feet in front of the wall, and smash the lob that comes back. A few minutes of smashing can be exhausting.

2. Ball machines are ideal for grooving strokes. Although the machine doesn't say "good shot," it puts the ball on a dime every time, right to a spot where you need practice, something no talking partner can do. When you're satisfied with your stroking standing still, move to the side between shots so you can take a few steps to the ball.

3. A bucket of balls can be a big ally on shots besides the serve and return of serve. To groove the ground strokes, repeatedly drop the ball out of your hand and hit it to spots on the court.

4. The most beneficial and sometimes most difficult way to groove strokes is to rally in patterns. Hit ground strokes cross court or down the line, concentrating on depth and pinpoint placement. Move one player to the net and practice any combination of cross-court and down-the-line volleys and passing shots. If you wish, aim for targets.

If you merely want to keep your strokes finely tuned, stroke-grooving drills are a good way to start a practice session. On the other hand, if a shot needs an overhaul, these exercises may comprise your whole workout.

In the basic stroke-grooving drills, down-the-line and cross-court balls are hit repeatedly. Here, the net man practices backhand volleys while the baseline player hits forehands down the line.

Movement Drills

1. In the "figure 8" drill, one player hits every shot cross court while the other player sends every shot down the line. If the players are steady, each moves constantly from side to side. An alternative is the "figure 6" drill, in which one

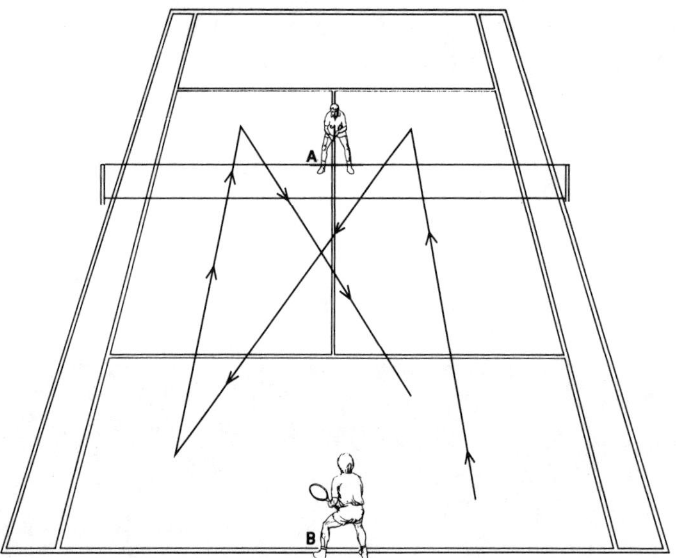

In the Figure 8 drill, Player A hits every ball cross court and Player B hits every ball down the line.

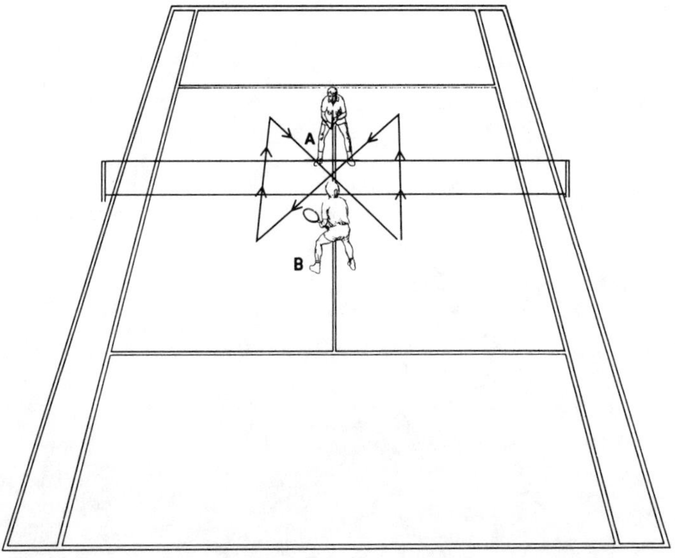

A variation of the Figure 8 drill has both players in at net hitting alternate forehand and backhand volleys.

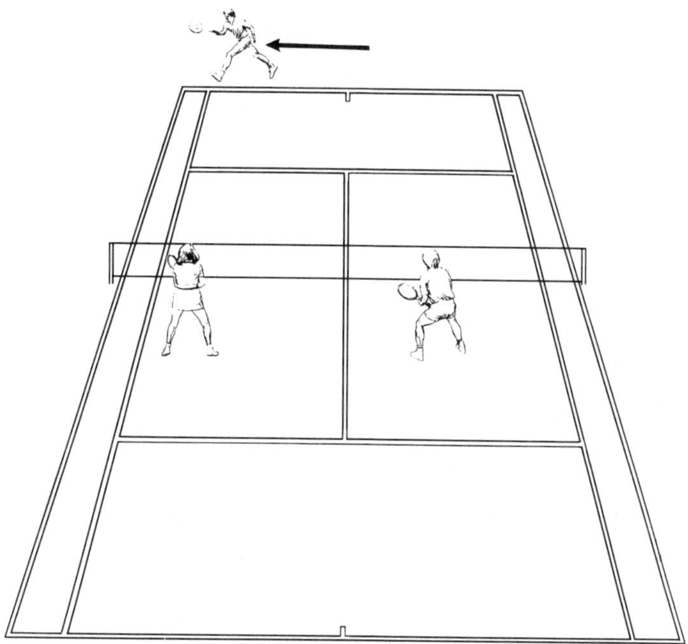

Two-on-one drills are invaluable for conditioning. They also train the player to hit the ball away from the center of the court.

player stays in a corner and alternates hitting cross court and down the line while the other scrambles back and forth.

2. Half-court drills are excellent for conditioning and sharpening strokes. A good one uses half the doubles court, one player standing at the net, the other on the baseline. The baseline player tries to pass or lob the net player. Since the court is 9 feet thinner than in singles, the net player gets to far more balls, forcing the backcourt player to hit pinpoint passing shots and lobs. In either down-the-line or cross-court half-court drills, both players will do a lot of running if the net player tries to put the ball away.

3. Two-on-one drills are a favorite of top players. In one of them, two players stand at the net, the third on the baseline. The volleyers run the baseline player as much as possible, refraining from putting the ball away, and the baseliner places ground strokes back to the net players. A variation puts one player at the net and two on the baseline, the pair hitting wide to make the net player run.

Match-Play Simulation. In this drill the "feeder," using a basket of balls, places a sequence of shots to simulate playing conditions.

4. In shot combination drills, one player, who is usually at the net, feeds two balls in a pattern to another player. A typical pattern would be a deep backhand, followed right away by a short forehand. You can add a third shot, such as a deep lob to the backhand, then a fourth, fifth, and so on. Any pattern and any number of shots can be used.

5. Since the "short-court scramble drill" is very rigorous and calls for continuous running, it should have a time limit, say one or two minutes. One player is at the net, the other inside the service line. The net player bunts the ball gently from side to side while the other player taps right to the net player. When time expires, the players switch roles.

Match-Play Drills

1. "Twenty-one" is a game played with table tennis scoring. There is no serving. Either player starts the rally by hitting the ball with a ground stroke. The ball must land in the court three times before the point begins. You are allowed to come to the net only on balls that land inside the service line. The first person to reach twenty-one points is the winner. The game emphasizes consistency on the ground strokes.

2. In "predetermined sets," the players must hit to certain spots on the court while playing sets. For example, you can specify that the server serve only to the backhand and the receiver direct every return to the server's forehand. After the serve and return, the points are played out normally.

3. Patterned drills can also be used to simulate common match-play situations. In one such exercise, two players hit a few ground strokes back and forth. Then one player intentionally hits the ball short and comes to net. The baseline player attempts a passing shot either down the line or cross court. Make note of patterns that arise in match play, and try to reproduce them in practice.

4. To practice closing on the volley, two players begin on their respective baselines and hit the ball back and forth in the air, moving closer to the net after each shot. After three or four shots, they should be volleying at close range.

List a number of drills in a notebook so you have plenty of exercises to choose from. Everybody tires of doing the same routines day in and day out.

Practicing is the only way to get better. Do it regularly, intensively, and enthusiastically.

Positive thinking throughout a match can help any player avoid choking.

12

Positive Thinking

In the preceding chapters, we discussed the strokes and tactics you'll need to become a strong player. There is more to playing good tennis, however, than a set of smooth strokes and the ability to map out an effective game plan. Thinking positively about the game is a large part of playing it correctly. There are two reasons why. First, one of the joys of tennis is extending and receiving the courtesies that are part of the game's long, proud tradition. Second, positive thinking helps you get the most out of your arsenal of strokes and tactics. It makes practice fun rather than drudgery and makes playing an exercise in finding a way to win instead of in staving off defeat. It prevents you from blowing your stack or tightening up under pressure and gives you a determined yet cool attitude that allows you to win with dignity. Your on-court behavior should help your matches go smoothly and pleasantly and impress opponents and spectators alike with your unflappable composure.

In this chapter, we discuss three aspects of positive thinking: sportsmanship, how to avoid choking, and how to get through periods when you're discouraged with tennis.

SPORTSMANSHIP

The term sportsmanship refers to your conduct on and around a tennis court. Some of the precepts of sportsmanship are quite vague, such as the ones that say you should "be gracious to your opponent" and "control your temper." Others are far more concrete—unwritten rules, in fact—falling into the area of sportsmanship known as etiquette. They include waiting until the point ends to walk across someone else's court, and shaking hands at the end of a match. In this section, we describe both the spirit and the letter of good sportsmanship.

Gone are the days when men played in long white-flannel pants and women in bloomers, when tennis was called the Sport of Kings. Today, the air of snobbery is gone and tennis is played at every social level, but the game retains an important legacy from its aristocratic beginnings. A few tantrum-prone stars and hackers aside, tennis players follow a strict code of conduct.

There are practical reasons for this, aside from tradition. First, some of the rules of tennis are foggy. For example, the book says "play shall be continuous" but doesn't tell you how many seconds you can take between points before you're stalling. So if you really want to, you can stall.

Second, even when the rules are clear, they're often hard to enforce. Most of you will be provided umpires and linesmen only when you're fortunate enough to get to the semifinals or finals of a tournament. If you foot-fault or take too much time between games, you'll be penalized. But most of the time you're on your own. You'd need binoculars to call your opponent for foot-faulting and a stopwatch for stalling. Players shouldn't tempt each other to make impossible calls; they should stick to the rules.

The better the sportsmanship, the more smoothly the match goes and the more likely it is to be decided by superior play rather than superior gamesmanship. In addition, if you're a good sport, you'll get a lot more invitations to play.

Let's look at the best way to behave before, during, and after a practice or tournament match.

Practice Etiquette

When you want to serve by yourself on undivided courts, pick a corner court if possible. That way, you can serve into the corner of the fence and keep the balls from disrupting play on the adjoining court. In addition, it is best not to practice with a bucket of balls on undivided courts. The balls will get mixed up, and everyone will waste a lot of time trying to straighten things out.

Your opponents, of course, are chosen for you in a tournament. But picking opponents to practice with can be sticky. If an equal or, better yet, a superior player asks you to play, say yes. You'll benefit. But what if the invitation comes from a weaker player? It's a good idea to accept occasionally. No one would ever improve if superior players were unwilling to sacrifice a little by practicing with lesser players. Up to a point, consider being unselfish, but don't expect everybody to be. If you ask a better player to play and get a lukewarm answer twice, stop asking.

Pre-Match Etiquette

Be on time. Otherwise you might end up leaving your partner pacing while your reservation time slips by, which can be annoying, particularly on expensive indoor courts. If you're often late, you'll have trouble keeping partners.

Although you needn't seek anyone out before a match, if you happen to run into your opponent, there is no reason not to be gracious. And don't make pre-match alibis; they may do more harm than good by putting you in a negative frame of mind. However, if you haven't been playing because of an injury, it is only fair to explain to your opponent that you may not be up to quite as good a game as usual. It's an apology, not an excuse. Don't say things like "I'd beat you as usual if I'd played in the last month."

If you have to cross an occupied court to get to your court, avoid walking behind the players during a rally. It's better to wait until it's over and signal to the players that you want to cross. Then, to keep the interruption short, run, don't stroll.

Leave dogs and children outside the fence. If you bring a van full of relatives who are baseball rather than tennis fans, tell them what is expected of tennis spectators.

When you get on the court, try to keep the warm-up short. Ten minutes or less is standard. Before a practice match, however, if you and your opponent agree to it, take half an hour or even longer to warm up.

During the warm-up, make sure both you and your opponent get as much practice as possible. Be steady. Everyone has run up against the opponent who monopolizes the net and puts away every volley. The battle starts with the first point, not the warm-up. Warm up all the shots, including volleys and overheads.

The rules say that you must practice serving during the warm-up only. Moreover, taking serves once the match has started, before the first game you serve, interrupts the flow of play.

Match Etiquette

Be careful not to "quick serve" accidentally, a term for serving before your opponent is ready. To make sure, pause just before starting your delivery.

When receiving, avoid inadvertently distracting the server by stamping your feet or "dancing." On the other hand, it's fine to shift your position slightly during the toss, even though it often draws a fault by luring the server into changing aim in mid-motion.

In a match involving beginners and intermediates, the server as official scorekeeper pauses on every point before the first delivery to announce the score. Otherwise, the players have a tendency to lose track. Experienced competitors, on the other hand, carefully keep score in their heads. In their matches, the server may call the score less often, about once every three points or so. If you are serving and lose count, consult your opponent; if your opponent has forgotten too, agree on a probable score.

Except on those rare occasions when linesmen are provided, you're responsible for calling your own lines. To avoid confusion, try to call every ball that's out, except the ones that hit the fence in the air and those so far out that you'd be rubbing salt in your opponent's wounds. Say "out" in a loud, clear voice—or "fault," if it's a serve.

Try to call the lines quickly, preferably right after the ball bounces. But don't sacrifice accuracy for hastiness. You'll have to return some balls before you can confidently call them out, especially service returns you take on the rise. On a soft court, take time, if need be, to check the ball mark.

If you don't see whether the ball is in or out, an unwritten rule says to call it in. You may not be able to judge because you're too far from the bounce, or because the net obstructs your view. In a practice match or an informal, club-style tournament, appeal to your partner. If he or she didn't see it either, the ball is in.

Most tennis players try hard to call the lines honestly. You can almost always trust your opponent's calls. The bounce on balls that land on the far side of the net is a lot easier to see over there. An opponent who inadvertently calls one or two of your "in" balls "out" is just as likely to call a couple of out balls in your favor. The outcome of the match is unaffected. But a tiny minority of players, out of dishonesty or ineptitude, make so many bad calls that the tide turns in their favor. If you meet one of these players in a social match, consider not playing with him or her again. If it's in a tournament, it's best to exercise your right to have a referee call the lines, no matter how embarrassed you are to do it. Above all, don't cheat back. Once a player is branded as a "hooker," a term for someone who cheats on calls, that player has trouble finding either tennis partners or tennis friends.

Gamesmanship

Gamesmanship, the art of stretching the rules to disrupt your opponent's concentration, is best left out of your game plan. Some common tricks you may face across the net include: an opponent who glares at you when you call a shot out, stalls by kicking and fumbling the balls between points, recites his or her medical history as you change sides, flatters you, and so on. These pranks often backfire, only inspiring you to try harder. On the other hand, complimenting an opponent sincerely with "good shot" or "nice try" can make a match much more pleasant.

Keeping Your Head

People play better when they keep their heads. Cursing and throwing a racket is in bad taste in the eyes of players and spectators alike. It disrupts your opponent's concentration, but it's twice as bad for you yourself. Although in every tough match there are stretches when a person gets unlucky or plays badly, it's better not to wallow in self-pity. Concentrate harder on the ball. It's a much more effective way of turning your luck around.

Concentrating and keeping your cool does not mean the same thing as being colorless. You can always exhort yourself by slapping your thigh or saying "Let's go!" It may even blow off a little steam and give you an attractive on-court personality. But given a choice, it's far better to be a complete poker face than a racket thrower.

Post-Match Etiquette

After the last point, whether you win or lose, try your best to shake hands cordially across the net with the other player. It's a nice touch to compliment your opponent's good game or sympathize with a poor one. A few words like "Nice match" or "I'm sure it'll be a lot closer next time" are usually appreciated. We all know the types who gloat or make excuses. It's particularly insulting when someone who just beat you says, "God, I played badly!"

When you're nearing the end of your reservation time while playing a practice match, be sensitive about when to yield the court to the next group of players. If you have a minute left, don't start a new game. On the other hand, if you are near the end of a long game when your time is up, the new group should let you finish it. Don't stay around for twelve deuces, however.

HOW TO AVOID CHOKING

Choking is the loss of rhythm on your strokes occurring when you're under pressure. Your swing tightens up, and you don't follow through. Strokes that were smooth in practice become jerky and cramped in a match. The serve and overhead, the strokes most susceptible to choking, degenerate into push shots. The sting goes out of the other shots as well. When you choke, the benefits of practice and experience desert you. The jerky style is an unfamiliar one.

Choking is the result of two things: uncertain strokes and negative thinking, specifically the fear of making a mistake. To avoid tightening up, you must firm up the strokes and replace fear with daring.

If you practice enough, good stroking becomes second nature and will surface every time you play. If a stroke is wobbly in practice, it inevitably gets worse in the tense atmosphere of a match.

But if your smooth, well-drilled shots choke up in a match, you need to change your thinking, not practice more. First, put the importance of the match in perspective. Tennis is, after all, a game. It's supposed to be fun. If you lose, no one's going to whip you, so why torture yourself?

Second, think about what you have to do to win rather than to avoid losing. Forget about your strokes and concentrate on your game plan. Before and during the match, visualize yourself moving through a point, picking on an opponent's backhand or executing another pattern. When you serve, don't think, "I've got to get the ball in or else," but rather, "I'm going to serve wide to that weak forehand." Assume your weapons are reliable, and focus on the strategy of winning the battle.

If you still feel yourself tightening, force yourself to play more aggressively. Come to the net more, hit harder serves and returns. Between points, take your time and breathe deeply.

As you build up a lead in a tough match, the tendency to choke increases. The daring you showed in forging ahead is replaced by ultraconservatism designed to protect your lead. When you're behind, on the other hand, you tend to loosen up with a "what the hell, I've got nothing to lose" attitude. Falling behind may help you by removing some of the pressure, or it may hinder you by making you reckless, as sure a way to lose as choking.

Don't be haunted by the specter of past mistakes. The missed setups and blown match points are history. And if you lose the first set, forget it. You start the second at 0–0, with a clean slate.

DEALING WITH DISCOURAGEMENT

Tennis can be discouraging for anyone, both the beginner straining to learn the game and the top player who just lost a tie breaker in the third set. At one time or another, all of us have wanted to give up. If you have poor strokes and are unwilling to change them, you'll experience the frustration of standing still and losing often. On the other hand, if you develop a solid foundation of strokes, tactics, and attitude, your upward progress, punctuated by only a few lulls, will keep you interested. The best way to keep from being discouraged, then, is to play properly.

Even if you are on the right track, discouragement may set in if you're practicing or playing either too much or not enough. When you play too much, you may get stale. Your enthusiasm wanes, and your sessions become drudgery rather than fun. The solution is simple: Take a few days off, and you won't have to push yourself to play anymore; you'll want to.

If you're playing too little, your strokes will get rusty. Shots you used to make with ease now misfire. Play every day until your shots return and the game becomes fun again.

Think positively about your tennis. Even when you're off on a side court covered with weeds, you're in a great tradition.

Appendix: Scoring

The basic rules for scoring the game of tennis are clearly spelled out by the United States Tennis Association. They read as follows:

The Game

If a player wins his first point, the score is called 15 for that player; on winning his second point, the score is called 30 for that player; on winning his third point, the score is called 40 for that player, and the fourth point won by a player is scored game for that player except as below:

If both players have won three points, the score is called deuce; and the next point won by a player is called advantage for that player. If the same player wins the next point, he wins the game; if the other player wins the next point the score is again called deuce; and so on until a player wins the two points immediately following the score at deuce, when the game is scored for that player. In matches played without an umpire the server should announce, in a voice audible to his opponent and spectators, the set score at the beginning of each game, and (audible at least to his opponent) point scores as the game goes on. Misunderstandings will be averted if this practice is followed.

The Set

A player (or players) who first wins six games wins a set; except that he must win by a margin of two games over his opponent and where necessary a set shall be extended until this margin be achieved. NOTE: See tie breaker.

The Tie Breaker

The tie breaker comes into play when games reach 6–all. The player whose turn it is to serve the next regular game is the first server. Call him Player A. He serves the first point into the right court, then Player B serves points 2 and 3, left court, right court. Player A serves points 4 and 5, left court, right court. Player B serves point 6, left court. Players change ends. Player B serves point 7, right court. The players continue to serve 2 points each in the same right/left pattern until the first player reaches a minimum of 7 points with a margin of 2. Players change ends after every 6 points.

Maximum Number of Sets

The maximum number of sets in a match shall be 5, or, where women take part, 3.

For those players who plan to compete regularly at the tournament level, we suggest a careful look at the whole USTA rule book. Doing so will save many needless arguments that do nothing but detract from the basic enjoyment of the game.